30

PASSAGES

30

PASSAGES

omprehension Practice for
igh Intermediate and Advanced Students

**Donn Byrne and
Edwin T. Cornelius, Jr.**

 **LONGMAN INC.**
New York

30 PASSAGES

First printing 1978

10   9   8   7   6

ISBN 0 582 79704 7

30 PASSAGES is the American English version of INTERMEDIATE COMPREHENSION PASSAGES, copyright © 1970, by Longman Group Ltd.

Illustrations and cover design by Tom Huffman

 Longman Inc.
95 Church Street
White Plains, N.Y. 10601

Distributed in the United Kingdom by Longman Group Ltd., Longman House, Burnt Mill, Harlow, Essex CM20 2JE, England, and by associated companies, branches and representatives throughout the world.

Printed in the U.S.A.

CONTENTS

SECTION TWO

Recall Exercises

SECTION THREE

Aural Comprehension Tests

INTRODUCTION

This book is intended for use with high intermediate-level and advanced students. It provides material for helping students improve their skills in comprehension of both written and oral material. The book is divided into three sections: reading passages, recall exercises and aural comprehension tests.

SECTION ONE consists of thirty reading passages with follow-up exercises. The passages increase in length and difficulty throughout the section, and the exercise material is carefully graded. At the beginning, emphasis is mainly on testing comprehension through multiple-choice questions. Gradually, however, the number of questions testing both comprehension and expression (performance) is increased, providing logical building blocks for composition work. Eight different types of exercises are used with the passages, including the following:

Multiple-choice questions (always Exercise A). Students should be asked to examine each alternative carefully because, in some cases, there is only a slight difference between the correct answer and wrong ones. The exercise is varied slightly throughout the section. With Passages 21 to 30, for example, students have to refer to the passage either to support a statement or to show why a particular statement is true or false.

Wh-type questions (always Exercise B). Students should be told to answer these questions with complete sentences, at least when the exercise is used for written practice. For example:
How long did it take them to load the boat?
It took them about thirty minutes to load the boat.

Questions and answers (Exercise C with Passages 1 to 20). Students should respond to these questions with short answers. For example:
Did they load the boat?
Yes, they did. (or No, they didn't.)

This particular exercise has two purposes: (1) to widen the range of comprehension testing, particularly of vocabulary items; and (2) to give students practice using short-answer forms. If the students' control of short-answer forms seems inadequate, the teacher may wish to devise additional question-answer drills.

Sentence completion (Exercise D with Passages 1 to 20, and Exercise C with Passages 21 to 30). In this exercise, students are required to restate some part of the passage in order to complete the sentences. The exercise, therefore, provides a test both of comprehension and expression (performance).

Word meaning (Exercise E with Passages 1 to 20, and Exercise D with Passages 21 to 30). With the first passages, students are asked to identify the meaning of general vocabulary items. With later passages, students have to refer to the passage to identify the meaning of words in particular contexts.

Matching exercise (Exercise F with Passages 11 to 20). Students are given a list of words and phrases, and are asked to refer to the reading passage to identify other words and phrases with similar or identical meaning.

Guided composition (Exercise F with Passages 1 to 10, Exercise G with 11 to 20, and Exercise E with 21 to 30). These exercises require students to write a short composition based on some point or feature in the reading passage. A specific assignment (add an ending, paraphrase a passage, etc.) is always given, and a word limit (90 words, 100 words, etc.) is always suggested.

Grammar notes and usage (Exercise G with Passages 1 to 10, Exercise H with 11 to 20, and Exercise F with 21 to 30). These exercises are always based on some point of usage taken from the reading passages. Brief explanatory notes with examples are given in most of the exercises.

SECTION TWO consists of Recall Exercises. These exercises are extracts from the reading passages in Section

One, but with certain structural features omitted or incomplete. They are intended as "recall" exercises and, therefore, should be assigned about a week after the corresponding reading passages have been completed. The exercises are arranged in four groups: verbs, articles, prepositions and adverbial particles, and linking words. A reference number is given after each individual exercise to indicate the relevant reading passage in Section One.

SECTION THREE contains two parts: Aural Comprehension Passages, and Dictation Passages. The comprehension passages usually relate (in theme and content) to two or three reading passages in Section One. There are ten comprehension passages, and the point at which each one should be used is indicated at the end of the passage. Checkup questions are given following each passage. The dictation passages given in the second part of the section also relate to the material in Section One. There are twelve dictation passages, and a reference is given with each one to indicate the point at which the dictation should be used.

SECTION ONE
COMPREHENSION PASSAGES

It was already late when we started out for the next town, which according to the map was about fifteen miles away on the other side of the hills. We felt sure that we would find a place to spend the night there. Darkness fell soon after we left, but luckily there were no other cars on the road as we drove quickly along the narrow winding road that led to the hills. As we climbed higher, it became colder and heavy rain began to fall, making it difficult at times to see the road clearly. I asked John to slow down.

After traveling for about twenty miles, there was still no sign of the town which was marked on the map. We were beginning to get worried. Then, without warning, the car stopped. We had run out of gas. Although we had very little to eat with us, only a few cookies and some candy bars, we decided to spend the night in the car.

Our "meal" was soon over. I settled down to go to sleep, but John was restless and after a few minutes he got out of the car and went for a walk up the hill. Soon he came running back. From the top of the hill, he had seen the lights of the town we were looking for. We quickly unloaded everything we could from the car, including our heavy suitcases and, with a great deal of effort, managed to push the car to the top of the hill. Then we went back for our baggage, loaded the car again and started coasting down the hill. In less than fifteen minutes, we were in the town, where we found a hotel quite easily.

5

10

15

20

25

A. *Choose the best answer.*

1. The travelers had a map but
   a. they did not know how to use it.
   b. it gave them the wrong information.
   c. they could not see it very well in the dark.
   d. the town they were looking for was not clearly marked.
2. Their car stopped because
   a. they had traveled more than twenty miles.
   b. they had run out of gas.
   c. they couldn't see the road.
   d. they were going uphill.

B. Answer the following questions briefly, using your own words as much as possible. Answer each question with a complete sentence.

1. What did the travelers expect to find in the next town?
2. How long did it take them to reach the town after they started coasting down the hill?

C. Answer these questions, using only short answers.

1. Was it dark when they left?
2. Did they find that it was easy to push the car uphill?

D. Complete the following sentences. Your answers must be related to the ideas contained in the reading passage.

1. The writer asked John to slow down because

   _____ .
2. John went for a walk because _____ .
3. "_____ ," said John, after he had run back to the car.
4. _____ so that it would be easier to push it to the top of the hill.
5. They would have spent the night in the car if

   _____ .

E. Choose the best explanation according to the story.

1. *winding* (6) means
   a. going uphill
   b. dangerous
   c. not straight
   d. cold
2. *without warning* (12) means
   a. suddenly
   b. nobody told them
   c. before it got hot
   d. without any explanation

F. Composition   Imagine that you are John. In your own words, describe what you did from the time you got out of the car until you reached the town. Limit your composition to 90 words, using only the ideas found in the reading passage.

G. *Look at this sentence:*

They *managed to* push the car to the top of the hill.
Manage(d) to + verb (main form) is a common way of
describing achievement—something successfully done,
often in spite of difficulties.

*Now rewrite these sentences, replacing the verb in
italics with the correct form of manage to* + verb.

1. My hat fell into the river, but I *succeeded in getting*
   it *out.*
2. Finally, after a long argument, we *were able to
   persuade* them.
3. He *succeeded in passing* his driving test, even
   though he is a bad driver.
4. *Were* you *able to find* the book you were looking for?
5. How on earth *did* you *succeed in finding out* where I
   live?
6. They *were able to put* the fire *out* before the whole
   house burned down.
7. No prisoner *has* ever *succeeded in escaping* from this
   prison.
8. If I'd *been able to get* some sleep, I wouldn't have felt
   so tired the next morning.
9. I can't understand how he *was able to stay* awake.
10. He gave a good excuse, but he *didn't* quite *succeed in
    convincing* me.

When I was walking down the street the other day, I happened to notice a small brown leather wallet lying on the sidewalk. I picked it up and opened it to see if I could find out the owner's name. There was nothing inside it except some change and an old photograph—a picture of a woman 5 and a young girl about twelve years old, who looked like the woman's daughter. I put the photograph back and took the wallet to the police station, where I handed it to the desk sergeant. Before I left, the sergeant took down my name and address in case the owner might want to write and thank 10 me.

That evening I went to have dinner with my aunt and uncle. They had also invited a young woman so that there would be four people at the table. Her face was familiar. I was quite sure that we had not met before, but I could not 15 remember where I had seen her. In the course of conversation, however, the young woman happened to mention that she had lost her wallet that afternoon. All at once I realized where I had seen her. She was the young girl in the photograph, although she was now much older. She 20 was very surprised, of course, when I was able to describe her wallet to her. Then I explained that I had recognized her from the photograph I had found in the wallet. My uncle insisted on going to the police station immediately to claim the wallet. As the police sergeant handed it over, he said 25 that it was an amazing coincidence that I had not only found the wallet, but also the person who had lost it.

A. Choose the best answer.

1. The wallet which the writer found
   a. was empty.
   b. had some money in it.
   c. had a few coins and a photograph in it.
   d. had an old photograph in it.
2. The writer recognized the young woman because
   a. he had met her somewhere before.
   b. she was the woman in the photograph.
   c. she often had dinner with his aunt and uncle.
   d. she resembled the young girl in the photograph.

B. *Answer the following questions briefly, using your own words as much as possible. Answer each question with a complete sentence.*
 1. Why did the sergeant take down the writer's name and address?
 2. Where did they go to get the wallet back?

C. *Answer these questions, using only short answers.*
 1. Did the writer find the owner's name in the wallet?
 2. Was the young woman surprised when the writer described her wallet?

D. *Complete the following sentences. Your answers must be related to the ideas contained in the reading.*
 1. When the writer opened the wallet, he expected to find _____.
 2. The sergeant had a note pad on which _____.
 3. The young woman _____ so that there would be four people at the table.
 4. The writer said, "There was a photograph in the wallet. That's how _____."
 5. "Let's _____," the writer's uncle insisted.

E. *Choose the best explanation according to the story.*
 1. *familiar* (14) means
    a. common
    b. known
    c. famous
    d. domestic
 2. *claim* (24) means
    a. pretend
    b. identify
    c. ask for
    d. take

F. *Composition*   Imagine that you are the young woman in the story. In no more than 90 words, describe what happened from the time you went to the house for dinner until you got your wallet back at the police station. Do not include any ideas other than those found in the reading passage. Use your own words as much as possible.

G. *Look at this sentence:*

The young woman *happened to mention* that she had lost her wallet.

This means: She *mentioned by chance* that she had lost her wallet. Similarly, I *happened to notice* means "I noticed by chance."

Now rewrite these sentences, replacing the verb in italics with happen to + *verb (main form).*

1. I was just coming out of the restaurant when I *saw* an old friend.
2. Betsy *said* she liked red roses, so George sent her a dozen of them.
3. I didn't hear about it until I *got* a letter from Henry.
4. That pen you found *is* mine.
5. He missed the beginning of the movie because he *got* there late.
6. We wanted to see Dr. Taylor, but he *wasn't* in his office.
7. If you *see* Laura, tell her to call me.
8. Do you *know* where Pete went this afternoon?
9. I'd like to lend you some money, but I don't *have* any with me.
10. The tree fell right across the highway, but luckily no one *was driving by* at the time.

August 31st

There are five people at our table, including myself. I've already learned a lot about them in the short time we've been at sea, although we rarely meet except at mealtimes.

First of all, there's Dr. Stone — my favorite, I must confess. 5
He's a man of about sixty-five, with gray hair and a pleasant face. He gave up his medical practice a short time ago and is traveling around the world before he retires to Florida. As a young man, he served overseas for a number of years as a doctor in the Navy. He speaks several languages and has 10
told us a lot about the port cities we're going to visit. He seems to have been everywhere. During the day, when he's not talking to other passengers (you get the impression he already knows everybody on board!), he sits on deck reading or looking out at sea through an old telescope. 15

Then there's "Grandma." I call her that because her name escapes me. In spite of being a grandmother, she looks remarkably young, not more than forty-five. She's on her way to visit a daughter who moved to Australia several years ago. Naturally, she's very excited at the thought of 20
seeing her daughter again, and of seeing her three grandchildren for the first time. She can talk of nothing else. This trip is quite an adventure for her since she has never been overseas before.

Then there's a man I don't like very much, a construction 25
engineer by the name of Barlow. He's been on leave in California and is now on his way back to the job he has in Singapore. He's very athletic and spends most of his time swimming or playing tennis. I've never in my life met a man with such a loud laugh. He has the cabin next to mine and I 30
can hear him laugh even through the thick cabin walls!

The other person who sits at our table is Mrs. Lang. I haven't found out very much about her yet. She's quiet and doesn't talk very much, except to consult with the doctor about her children's various ailments. She's on her way to 35
join her husband in Bangkok.

A. Choose the best answer.

1. Dr. Stone is traveling around the world because
   a. he likes meeting a lot of people.
   b. he wants to do some traveling before he retires.
   c. he wants to visit the places he was in years ago.
   d. he enjoys traveling overseas.
2. The writer calls the second person at the table "Grandma" because
   a. she looks old.
   b. she has three grandchildren.
   c. he has never known her name.
   d. he has forgotten her name.

B. Answer the following questions briefly, using your own words as much as possible. Answer each question with a complete sentence.

1. How does Dr. Stone spend his time when he is not talking to other passengers?
2. Why is "Grandma" going to Australia?

C. Answer these questions, using only short answers.

1. Does the writer spend a lot of time with the people who eat at his table?
2. Is "Grandma" the oldest person at the table?

D. Complete the following sentences. Your answers must be related to the ideas contained in the reading passage.

1. Dr. Stone _____ after he has gone around the world.
2. Dr. Stone seems to know everyone on board because _____.
3. Barlow spends most of his time _____.
4. Barlow has such a loud laugh that _____.
5. The writer does not know much about Mrs. Lang because _____.

E. Choose the best explanation according to the story.

1. *remarkably* (18) means
   a. attractively
   b. quite
   c. noticeably
   d. extraordinarily

2. *on leave* (26) means
   a. about to go
   b. away from one's job
   c. absent
   d. at home

F. Composition   In about 75 words, write an imaginary description of the writer of this diary. Make it read like an entry from a diary of your own.

G. Look at these sentences:
   We *rarely* meet except at mealtimes.
   I can *never* remember her name.
   She has *never* been overseas before.
Frequency adverbs (answering the question "How often?") are usually placed in front of the main verb in the sentence. Here are examples of frequency adverbs in a question and a negative statement:
   Does it *often* rain in March?
   He didn't *always* finish his reading assignments.
Common adverbs of this kind are *always, never, often, seldom, usually, generally, sometimes.*
Adverbials such as *every day (every week, every month . . .), once (twice, . . .) a day (month, year, . . .)* are usually placed at the end of the sentence:
   He buys a newspaper *every morning.*
   She has to see the doctor *twice a month.*

Now complete the following sentences by putting the frequency adverbs in the correct position.
   1. I get home later when I take the bus. *(usually)*
   2. Does Helen stay out late at night? *(often)*
   3. The mailman brings the mail at eight o'clock. *(every morning)*
   4. My paintings are exhibited in art galleries. *(seldom)*
   5. He writes to his parents. *(three times a year)*
   6. She doesn't shout at the children. *(generally)*
   7. When I'm involved in something, I forget the time. *(always)*
   8. Who walks to class with you in the morning? *(sometimes)*
   9. He worked hard when he was a young man. *(never)*
   10. Do you drink a lot of iced tea in hot weather? *(usually)*

11

Half an hour before daybreak, three of the boys met, as agreed, near the old bridge. The fourth, a boy by the name of Brian, had not turned up. No one was surprised that he wasn't there because they knew that his mother did not want him to come on this camping trip to the woods.   5

Frank, who was the oldest and the group's accepted leader, waded downstream to the place where their boat was tied up in the shelter of some overhanging bushes. Then he rowed the boat back to the shallow water near the bridge, where the boys loaded it with the food, blankets and other   10 things they were taking on their trip.

Dawn was just breaking as they climbed into the boat and pushed off from the bank. A swift current carried them downstream, so there was no need to row. They took turns keeping the boat towards the middle of the river. Three   15 hours later they entered the woods where they intended to spend the next few days.

"Let's go ashore now and fix some lunch," suggested Frank. "This looks like a good spot."

While Frank tied up the boat, the other two boys started   20 gathering wood for a fire. When they came back, each with a little kindling and an armload of wood, they found Frank looking very worried.

"We don't have any matches," he announced gloomily.
"Brian was supposed to bring them." 25

This was bad news. They were miles away from home now.

A. *Choose the best answer.*

1. The boys did not have to row because
   a. they had plenty of time to get to the woods.
   b. they kept their boat in the middle of the river.
   c. the river carried their boat along because of the
      fast current.
   d. they had pushed off from the bank.
2. The boys could not light a fire because
   a. the wood was wet.
   b. Frank had forgotten to bring matches.
   c. building a fire in the woods was prohibited.
   d. the boy who was going to bring the matches had
      not come on the camping trip.

B. *Answer the following questions, using your own words as much as possible. Answer each question with a complete sentence.*

1. How long did it take them to load the boat?
2. When did Frank discover that they had no matches?

C. *Answer these questions, using only short answers.*

1. Was it light when they set off downstream?
2. Did Frank go to gather wood too?

D. *Complete the following sentences. Your answers must be related to the ideas contained in the reading passage.*

1. The name of the boy who _____ was Brian.
2. It was easier to load the boat near the bridge because
   _____.
3. The boys did not have to row because there was
   _____ which _____.
4. While they were traveling downstream, all the boys
   had to do was _____.
5. After they had traveled for about three hours, the
   boys _____.

E. Choose the best explanation according to the story.

1. *waded* (7) means
   a. crossed the river
   b. swam
   c. went out of sight
   d. walked through the water
2. *took turns* (14) means
   a. went around and around
   b. one after the other
   c. all together
   d. from time to time

F. Composition

Imagine that you are Frank. Describe in no more than 90 words what you did from the time you waded downstream to get the boat until you discovered that you had no matches. Use your own words as much as possible, but do not introduce any ideas not included in the reading.

G. Look at this sentence:

The other two boys *started gathering* wood for a fire. In this pattern, the verb *start* is followed by the -*ing* form (sometimes referred to as a *gerund*) of another verb. Here are two more examples:

Would you *mind talking* in a lower voice?
The children *enjoyed playing* in the park.

Now complete the following sentences by choosing an appropriate verb from the list given below.

wash	paint	race
get	rain	watch
overhear	send	wear
make		

1. Let's go for a walk as soon as it stops _____ .
2. They kept on _____ a lot of noise even after I asked them to stop.
3. Mary never minds _____ the dinner dishes.
4. She begged her husband to give up _____ motorcycles on weekends.

5. I don't remember _____ you a Christmas card last year.
6. My grandfather enjoys _____ television.
7. I can't imagine _____ such a heavy coat on a hot day!
8. I couldn't help _____ what you said about me.
9. Why on earth did you suggest _____ the car red?
10. Have you ever considered _____ a job overseas?

The children stopped chattering as Miss Rios entered the classroom. Then in a loud chorus, they said, "Good morning, teacher."

Miss Rios smiled, said good morning and glanced quickly around the room. There seemed to be about thirty-five in the 5 class—perhaps a few more girls than boys. All of the children were watching her intently, waiting no doubt to find out what sort of person she was. "I suppose you want to know my name," she said.

But before she could tell them, someone in the class called 10 out, "You're Miss Rios." Everybody laughed. Miss Rios laughed too.

"News travels fast," she said. "I'm afraid it will take me longer to learn all your names."

Miss Rios opened her attendance book and called their 15 names one by one. When she came to the last name on the list, John Young, she noticed that he had been absent for over a month.

"What's the matter with John Young?" she asked, looking up. 20

"He's in the hospital, Miss Rios," said a dark-haired girl in the front row. "He broke his leg."

"He was ice-skating," added one of the boys.

"Has anyone been to the hospital to see him?" Miss Rios asked. 25

No one replied.

It was time to get started. "Now let me see," said Miss Rios, looking at her class schedule. "The first subject is English."

"Oh! Please read us a story," begged one of the girls. 30

Several of the children echoed this request. Miss Rios smiled.

"All right," she said. "But first of all, I want you to write a short letter to John Young. We'll send the letters to him in the hospital to cheer him up. Afterwards, I'll read you a 35 story."

They were all writing and drawing busily when Miss Rios slipped out of the room to get a book she had left in the teachers' lounge. She passed the Principal in the hall.

"Any problems with that class?" the Principal asked.

"Not so far," said Miss Rios confidently. "They all seem very well behaved."

A. Choose the best answer.

1. Miss Rios came into the classroom
   a. but nobody paid any attention to her.
   b. and a few of the children said good morning to her.
   c. and all the children said good morning.
   d. and all the children stood up at the same time.
2. Miss Rios
   a. refused to read a story to the class.
   b. had forgotten her attendance book, so she asked the class to write a letter.
   c. asked the class to write a letter before she read them a story.
   d. asked the class to write a letter so that she could go to the teachers' lounge.

B. Answer the following questions in your own words. Answer each question with a complete sentence.

1. Why did Miss Rios say, "News travels fast"?
2. What did Miss Rios do in order to find out who was absent?

C. Answer these questions, using only short answers.

1. Was Miss Rios a new teacher?
2. Did Miss Rios have any trouble with the class?

D. Complete the following sentences. Your answers must be related to the ideas contained in the reading.

1. After greeting the class, Miss Rios said, "_____."
2. No one replied when Miss Rios asked whether
   _____.
3. Miss Rios looked at the schedule in order to find out
   _____.
4. Miss Rios said that she wanted the class to write to John Young before _____.
5. Miss Rios met the Principal while _____.

E. Choose the best explanation according to the story.

1. *intently* (7) means
   a. with a great deal of attention
   b. by chance
   c. on purpose
   d. unpleasantly

2. *not so far* (41) means
   a. very near
   b. very much
   c. to a small degree
   d. not up to now

F. Composition
Imagine that you are Miss Rios. In your own words, describe what you did from the time you opened the attendance book until you went out of the classroom. Do not introduce ideas which are not included in the reading passage. Limit your composition to 90 words.

G. Look at this sentence:

She noticed that he *had been* absent for over a month.
The Past Perfect tense is commonly used to show that one event or action in the past occurred before another event or action also in the past. Here is another example:

Miss Rios slipped out to get a book (that) she *had left* in the teachers' lounge.
The Present Perfect becomes the Past Perfect in indirect speech after a reporting verb *(ask, say, tell,* etc.) in the past tense. For example:

Miss Rios *asked* whether anyone *had been* to see John Young.
The Past Perfect is also used in the *if*-clause of a conditional sentence, such as:

I would have helped you if you *had asked* me to.

Now complete the following sentences by changing the verbs in parentheses to the Past Perfect tense.

1. He went to the police station with a wallet that he _____ *(find)* on the sidewalk.

2. Helen admitted that she _____ (not, read) the assignment very carefully.
3. By the end of the year, they _____ (save) two hundred dollars.
4. Miss Rios would have gone back to the classroom immediately if she _____ (hear) any noise.
5. They wrote to say that they _____ already _____ (buy) a house.
6. If the children _____ (be) a problem, I would have told you.
7. I went to see my friend who _____ just _____ (come back) from overseas.
8. By the time Bill got to the drugstore, he _____ (forgot) what he wanted to buy.
9. How long did it take you to realize that you _____ (see) that movie already?
10. She would have missed her appointment if the bus _____ (be) a few minutes late.

    Bill Fuller, the mailman, whistled cheerfully as he walked up the hill towards Mrs. Carter's house. His work for the day was almost finished; his bag, usually quite heavy when he started out on his rounds, was empty now except for the letter that he had to deliver to Mrs. Carter. She lived quite a   5 few blocks away, so when Bill had mail for her, he always finished his day's work much later. He did not mind this, though, because she never failed to ask him in for coffee and a piece of her special spice cake.

    When Bill got to Mrs. Carter's house, he was surprised not   10 to find her working in the yard. She usually spent her afternoons there when the weather was good. Bill went around to the back of the house, thinking that she might be in the kitchen. The door was locked and the curtains were drawn. Puzzled, he returned to the front of the house and   15 knocked loudly on the front door. There was no answer. Bill thought that this was very strange because he knew that Mrs. Carter rarely left the house.

    Just then he noticed that her bottle of milk, which is always delivered early in the morning, was still on the   20 porch. This worried him. If Mrs. Carter had not taken in her milk, maybe she was sick. Bill walked around the house

until he found an open window. It was a small window, but
he managed to squeeze through. He went into the hall.
There he almost stumbled over Mrs. Carter, who was lying   25
unconscious at the foot of the stairs. Realizing that he
needed to get help, and knowing that there was no telephone
there, he rushed out of the house, stopped a passing car and
told the driver to go to the nearest telephone and call an
ambulance.   30

A. *Choose the best answer.*
   1. Bill Fuller was going to Mrs. Carter's house because
      a. she had invited him for coffee and cake.
      b. he had a package to deliver to her.
      c. his day's work was over.
      d. he had a letter for her.
   2. The thing that worried Bill the most was
      a. finding the back door locked and the curtains
         drawn.
      b. seeing her bottle of milk on the porch.
      c. not getting any answer when he knocked on the
         door.
      d. not finding Mrs. Carter in the front yard.

B. *Answer the following questions in your own words.*
   Answer each question with a single complete sentence.
   1. How did Bill get into the house?
   2. How did Bill get help for Mrs. Carter?

C. *Answer these questions, using only short answers.*
   1. Was Bill riding his bicycle up the hill?
   2. Was Mrs. Carter alive when Bill found her?

D. *Complete the following sentences. Your answers must*
   be related to the ideas contained in the reading.
   1. Bill's bag was not heavy because _____ .
   2. When the weather was good, Mrs. Carter _____ .
   3. Bill was worried when he saw that _____ .
   4. It was lucky that one of the windows was open,
      otherwise _____ .
   5. As soon as Bill got into the house, he _____ , where
      he found Mrs. Carter _____ .

E. Choose the best explanation according to the story.

1. *did not mind* (7) means
   a. looked forward to
   b. enjoyed
   c. did not remember
   d. did not object to
2. *the curtains were drawn* (14) means
   a. they were wrinkled
   b. somebody had drawn
      pictures on them
   c. they were closed
   d. they were open

F. Composition
Imagine that you are Bill. In your own words, describe what you did from the time you got to Mrs. Carter's house until you rushed out of the house to get help. Do not introduce any ideas that are not included in the reading. Limit your composition to 90 words.

G. Look at this sentence:
His bag was usually *quite* heavy when he started out. The meaning of *quite* here is "moderately"—that is, his bag was not excessively heavy, but it was not light either. In this sense, *quite* is often close in meaning to "fairly" or "rather," depending on the context. In conversation, we also use *pretty* to indicate this.

Now complete the following sentences by choosing an appropriate word or phrase from the list given below. Note the different ways in which quite *is used.*

a while ago	deep	sure
a few	used to	possible
a young lady	interesting	often
crowded		

1. The restaurant was quite _____, but we managed to find a table near the door.
2. According to the radio, it is quite _____ that we will have rain tomorrow.
3. There were quite _____ people at the meeting— twenty to twenty-five, at least.

4. I'm tired. I'm not quite _____ that I want to go to a movie tonight.

5. The water is shallow here, but near the bridge it is quite _____.

6. They go to town quite _____, at least twice a week.

7. It was quite an _____ lecture, but I enjoyed the one yesterday much more.

8. I'll be sorry to leave this place. I've grown quite _____ it.

9. Your daughter has really grown up. She's quite _____ now!

10. I can't remember exactly when we were there, but I know that it was quite _____.

Lydia packed a small suitcase, said goodbye to her mother and hurried out of the house to catch the bus to the station. There was no one else waiting at the bus stop, so it looked as if a bus had just gone by. Lydia looked at her watch and frowned; it was already two o'clock. Her train left at 5 two-thirty, and since it would take at least twenty minutes to get to the station, she did not have much time to spare, even if a bus came along right away.

Just then a taxi came around the corner and moved slowly toward her. Lydia knew that the fare to the station was at 10 least four dollars, which was more than she could afford; but she quickly made up her mind that it would be well worth the extra expense in order to be sure of catching her train. So she waved down the taxi and got in. She told the driver that she had to catch a two-thirty train. He nodded and said 15 that he would take a shortcut to get her to the station in time.

All went well until, just as they were coming out of a side street into the main avenue that led to the station, the taxi ran into a car. There was a loud crash and Lydia was thrown 20 forward so violently that she hit her head on the front seat. Both drivers got out and began shouting at each other. Then

Lydia got out and asked them to stop arguing, but neither of them paid any attention to her.

Lydia was now quite sure that she was going to miss her train, even though she was not very far from the station. She was wondering what to do when a bus came along, heading in the direction of the station. The bus stop was just at the next corner, so Lydia got her suitcase out of the taxi and ran towards the bus, which had stopped to leave some passengers off. The bus driver saw her running and waited for her. Lydia got to the station just in time and managed to catch her train after all.

25

30

A. Choose the best answer.

1. Lydia took a taxi because
   a. she was afraid of missing her train.
   b. she was tired of waiting for the bus.
   c. it was already two-thirty.
   d. she had a heavy suitcase to carry.
2. As it turned out, Lydia
   a. arrived at the station in a taxi.
   b. did not reach the station.
   c. took the bus part of the way.
   d. had to walk most of the way to the station.

B. Answer the following questions in your own words with a single complete sentence.

1. Why did Lydia think that she had just missed the bus?
2. What happened to Lydia when the taxi ran into a car?

C. Answer these questions, using only short answers.

1. Did Lydia know how much it cost to go to the station by taxi?
2. Did Lydia stop to pay the taxi driver?

D. Complete the following sentences. Your answers must be related to the ideas contained in the reading.

1. The train that Lydia _____ left at two-thirty.
2. Lydia did not usually go to the station by taxi because _____ .

3. The taxi driver nodded and said, "_____."
4. The bus had stopped at the corner so that _____ .
5. If the bus driver had not seen her running, Lydia
_____ .

E. *Choose the best explanation according to the story.*
1. *right away* (8) means
   a. on the right side of
      the street
   b. at once
   c. from any direction
   d. in the opposite direction
2. *shortcut* (16) means
   a. interruption
   b. most direct route
   c. secret path
   d. back street

F. *Composition*   Imagine that you are Lydia. In your own words, describe what you did from the time the taxi came along until you caught the bus. Do not include any ideas that are not in the reading passage. Limit your composition to 100 words.

G. In the reading, there are several examples of *to* + verb (main form) used to express purpose; for example:
   Lydia hurried out of the house *to catch* the bus.
In order to + verb may be used to express the same idea.
   It would be well worth the extra expense *in order to be* sure . . .
The negative form is *in order not to* + verb.
   He hurried as fast as he could *in order not to be* late.

Now look at the following pairs of sentences. In each case, combine the two sentences to form a single sentence. Follow the examples given above.
1. I put on my glasses. I wanted to read the small print in the contract.
2. She's going for a walk. She wants to get some fresh air.
3. He deliberately crossed the street. He didn't want to speak to me.

4. I have to go to the library. I want to look up some information on pesticides.
5. He's gone to the bank. He wants to cash a check.
6. They went to a small hotel. They didn't want to spend a lot of money.
7. We should leave now. We want to be sure of getting a seat.
8. I must stop at the drugstore. I want to buy some cough medicine.
9. John went to the airport. He wanted to see his brother off.
10. I'm going to turn the music down. I don't want to disturb the others.

IT DOESN'T PAY TO WRITE

A car pulled up outside the Driftwood Motel and a young man got out. Pausing only for an instant to make sure that he had come to the right place, he went into the motel office and rang the bell on the counter to attract somebody's attention.

Mrs. Crenshaw, the motel manager, who was busy in the kitchen at that moment, hurried out, wiping her hands on a towel. The young man raised his hat.

"Excuse me," he said. "I'm looking for my uncle, Mr. Mancini. I believe he's staying here."

"He *was* staying here," Mrs. Crenshaw corrected him. "But I'm afraid that he went back to San Francisco yesterday."

"Oh, no!" said the young man, looking disappointed. "I understood that he was going to be here until the end of the month. At least that's what they told me when I called his office."

"That's right," said Mrs. Crenshaw. "He had intended to stay here the whole month of July, as he always does. But yesterday he got a telegram saying that one of his relatives was seriously ill. So he took a flight back to San Francisco immediately."

"I wish he had let me know," the young man said. "I wrote him a letter saying that I was coming. Now I've made this long trip for nothing. Well, since he isn't here, there's no point in waiting."

He thanked Mrs. Crenshaw and went out. Mrs. Crenshaw went to the window and watched him drive off. As soon as his car was out of sight, she called out, "You can come out now, Mr. Mancini. He's gone."

Mr. Mancini came out of the kitchen, where he had been waiting.

"Thanks very much, Mrs. Crenshaw," he said, laughing. "You did that very well. These nephews of mine never give me any peace. That young man is the worst of them all. As you see, when he needs money, he goes to great lengths to find me. Well, maybe next time he won't warn me in advance by writing a letter!"

A. Choose the best answer.

1. This story is about a man who
   a. did not like his nephew.
   b. did not want to see his nephew.
   c. was not able to see his nephew.
   d. wanted to spend a month at an ocean resort.
2. When his nephew came to the motel, the man
   a. avoided discussing the subject of money.
   b. caught a flight back to San Francisco.
   c. went to see a sick relative.
   d. hid in the kitchen.

B. Answer the following questions in your own words, using a simple complete sentence for each.

1. How did Mrs. Crenshaw know that someone had come into the motel office?
2. Why did Mrs. Crenshaw watch the young man drive off?

C. Answer these questions, using only short answers.

1. Had the young man come to the right motel?
2. Had Mr. Mancini stayed in this particular motel before?

D. Complete the following sentences. Your answers must be related to the ideas contained in the reading.

1. When Mrs. Crenshaw heard the bell ring, _____ .
2. The young man came to the Driftwood Motel expecting _____ .
3. The young man was disappointed when he heard that

   _____ .
4. Mr. Mancini did not come out of the kitchen until

   _____ .
5. Mr. Mancini thanked Mrs. Crenshaw for _____ .

E. Choose the best explanation according to the story.

1. *pulled up* (1) means
   a. waited
   b. stopped
   c. paused
   d. appeared

2. *no point in* (25) means
   a. no time to
   b. boring
   c. unnecessary
   d. unimportant

F. Composition   Imagine that you are Mr. Mancini. In your own words, describe the scene that took place between your nephew and Mrs. Crenshaw. Do not introduce any ideas which are not included in the reading passage. Limit your composition to 100 words.

G. Look at this sentence:

Mrs. Crenshaw went to the window and *watched* him *drive off.*

In this pattern, a verb of perception (*see, hear, feel, notice,* etc.) is followed by an object (noun or pronoun) + the main form of the verb (without *to*). The use of the main form of the verb (without *to*) here indicates completed action. Here is another example:

I *heard* the bell *ring.* (The bell rang. I heard it.)

This pattern (verb without *to*) is also used with a number of other verbs: *make, let, help.*

She *made (let, helped)* her husband *cut down* the tree. Compare verb without *to* with the pattern in which verb-*ing* is used (see Exercise F on page 107). The use of the -*ing* form of a verb in this pattern indicates that the action is still going on (continuing).

Now complete these sentences by choosing an appropriate verb from the list. Use the verb without *to* pattern or verb-*ing*.

change	go out	say
fall to	happen	slip from
finish	jump over	wash
fly out of	speak	

1. He closed the door quietly so that no one would hear him _____ .
2. Who actually saw the accident _____ ?
3. Do you know what made her _____ her mind?
4. Just watch me _____ that wall.

5. Let me _____ what I'm saying before you interrupt.
6. Nobody offered to help Joan _____ the dishes.
7. Did anyone notice the bird _____ its cage?
8. I've never heard her _____ a kind word about anybody.
9. He felt the heavy box _____ his hands and _____ the ground.
10. Have you ever heard him _____ Spanish?

7910 Gunther Street
Bellevue, Washington 98005
October 10th

Dear Rosemary,

I was delighted to get your letter this morning. I really 5
should have written to you several weeks ago — I owed you
a letter, I know—but I've been terribly busy. The children
seem to take up all of my time. Ann will be five next month
and I'm thinking of sending her to nursery school. Our little
one has just started walking and doesn't give me a moment's 10
peace. But you know what it's like! How are all your
children? They must love living in the country!

I'm afraid we can't come to see you next weekend, as you
suggested. Tom's mother is coming to spend the day with us
on Sunday. What about the weekend after this one — the 15
22nd and 23rd? We're free that weekend and would love to
come. We're anxious to see your new house.

Let me know if that weekend would be all right. We would
plan on leaving there fairly early Sunday afternoon to miss
the heavy traffic coming back. Can we bring anything? 20

Love from all of us,
Edna

Route 1, Box 10
Cheverton, Washington 98021
October 15th 25

Dear Edna,

Yes, we'd love to have you come the weekend of the 22nd
and 23rd! And please try to get here as early as you can on
Saturday. We'll plan on having lunch around noon. Ted says
that Tom can help him plant some birch trees out back. He 30
wasn't terribly excited when I said that the children would
help too! I'm looking forward to seeing the baby. Is he really
walking already? Time certainly flies!

We've had a lot of work to do on the house, but it's been
worth it. It's good to be living in the country again. I never 35
really enjoyed city life, as you know. You ought to look for a
place in the country. It's a completely different way of life

and I'll bet you'd enjoy it. But I suppose Tom wouldn't like commuting every day.

We'll expect you by noon on Saturday the 22nd. Take care 40
of yourself and don't work too hard!

Love to you all,
Rosemary

A. Choose the best answer.

1. Edna could not go to see Rosemary the following weekend because
   a. she was afraid of the traffic.
   b. Tom's mother was coming to see them that Sunday.
   c. she preferred to come the next weekend.
   d. she was terribly busy with the children.
2. Rosemary said "Time certainly flies" because
   a. Edna was coming to see them the weekend after next.
   b. she had never seen the baby.
   c. there was not enough time to do all the work in the house.
   d. she could hardly believe that the baby could walk already.

B. Answer the following questions in your own words. Answer each question with a single complete sentence.

1. How soon did Edna answer Rosemary's letter?
2. How were Edna and Tom going to get to the country?

C. Answer these questions, using only short answers.

1. Had Edna already seen Rosemary's new house in the country?
2. Had Rosemary lived in the country before?

D. Complete the following sentences. Your answers should be related to the ideas contained in the reading.

1. Edna had not had time to answer Rosemary's letter because _____.
2. Edna wrote to say that they could not come the following weekend because _____.
3. Edna suggested instead that _____.

4. Ted did not want the children _____ .

5. At the end of her letter, Rosemary told Edna

_____ .

E. Choose the best explanation according to the letters.
  1. *terribly* (7) means
      a. extremely
      b. unusually
      c. frighteningly
      d. unpleasantly
  2. *commuting* (39) means
      a. talking to neighbors
      b. being lonely
      c. substituting
      d. driving to and from
          the city

F. Composition   Imagine that you are Edna. Write a
  letter to a friend describing your weekend in the country
  with Rosemary and Ted. In your letter, refer to the
  house, Ted's birch trees, the meals and the trip back to
  Bellevue on Sunday evening. Limit your composition to
  100 words.

G. Look at this sentence:
      I really *should have written* to you.
  Should or *ought to* with the Present Perfect (*have* + past
  participle) is used to express an obligation which was
  not carried out. Here is another example:

  Helen $\begin{Bmatrix} should \\ ought\ to \end{Bmatrix}$ *have gone* to the dentist yesterday

  (but she didn't go).
  The negative form expresses disapproval of an action
  which was actually performed.
      You *shouldn't (ought not to) have bought* that hat.

  Now complete these sentences.
      1. This meat isn't done. You should _____ *(cook)* it
          longer.
      2. We'll miss the train. We ought to _____ *(leave)*
          earlier.
      3. Why did you let her go alone? Someone should
          _____ *(go)* with her.

4. I'm surprised he did that. He ought to _____ (know) better.
5. The accident was his fault. He shouldn't _____ (be driving) so fast.
6. You ought to _____ (ask) their permission before you borrowed it.
7. We should _____ (bring) a map. Now we're lost.
8. All my shirts are dirty. They should _____ (be sent) to the laundry yesterday.
9. They ought not to _____ (sell) their house. Now they don't have anyplace to live.
10. It's too late now. I should _____ (be told) the story earlier.

In November of last year, my brother and I were invited to spend a few days with an uncle who had just returned from overseas. He had a cabin in the mountains, although he seldom spent much time there. We understood the reason for this after our arrival. The cabin had no comfortable　　5 furniture in it, several of the windows were broken and the roof leaked—making the whole place damp and uninviting.

On our first evening, we sat around the fire after supper listening to stories our uncle had to tell of his many adventures overseas. I was so tired after the long trip that I　　10 would have preferred to go to bed, but I did not want to miss any of my uncle's exciting stories.

He was just in the middle of describing a terrifying experience he once had in a small sailboat out on the ocean during a storm, when there was a loud crash from the　　15 bedroom upstairs—the one where my brother and I were going to sleep.

"It sounds like the roof caved in!" exclaimed my uncle, with a loud laugh.

When we got to the top of the stairs and opened the　　20 bedroom door, we could not see anything at first because of the clouds of dust that filled the room. When the dust began to settle, we saw a strange sight. Part of the roof had fallen in and broken boards, shingles and huge chunks of plaster had come down on my bed. I was glad that I had stayed up　　25 late to listen to my uncle's stories; otherwise, I would have been seriously injured, or perhaps even killed.

That night we all slept on the floor in the big room downstairs, not wanting to risk our lives sleeping upstairs under a roof that might collapse on our heads. We left for　　30 home the next morning and my uncle gave up his cabin in the mountains. This was not the kind of adventure he was looking for!

A. Choose the best answer.

1. The writer did not go to bed immediately after supper because
   a. it was pleasant sitting around the fire.
   b. his uncle terrified him with his stories.

c. he wanted to hear all of his uncle's exciting stories.

d. his uncle made him listen to his stories.

2. It was certain that the ceiling had fallen in

   a. when they opened the bedroom door.

   b. after the dust had begun to clear.

   c. as soon as they heard the crash.

   d. when they reached the head of the stairs.

B. *Answer the following questions in your own words.*
Answer each question with a single complete sentence.

1. Why didn't the writer's uncle spend much time in his cabin?

2. Why were they afraid to sleep upstairs that night?

C. *Answer these questions, using only short answers.*

1. Was the writer's uncle amused when he heard the loud crash?

2. Did the writer's uncle continue living in his cabin?

D. *Complete the following sentences. Your answers must be related to the ideas contained in the reading.*

1. The writer's uncle did not spend much time in the cabin which _____ .

2. The cabin was damp because _____ .

3. Although the writer was tired, _____ .

4. _____ right onto the pillow of the bed where

_____ .

5. If the writer had gone to bed early, _____ .

E. *Choose the best explanation according to the story.*

1. *leaked* (7) means

   a. was beginning to fall down

   b. needed to be repaired

   c. let the rain in

   d. was in bad condition

2. *injured* (27) means

   a. badly hurt

   b. struck

   c. damaged

   d. wounded

F. *Composition*   Imagine that you are the writer's uncle. Write a short account of the experience you had when your sailboat was carried out to sea in a storm. Limit your composition to 120 words.

G. *Look at this sentence:*

I was glad that I had stayed up late to listen to my uncle's stories; *otherwise*, I would have been seriously injured.

Here the conjunction *otherwise* is replacing *If I hadn't stayed up late*. You can avoid repetition by using this conjunction. Here are some more examples:

Be quiet!   *Otherwise* (if you are not quiet), I won't tell you a story.

You'll have to work harder; *otherwise* (if you don't work harder), you won't pass the examination.

Now combine the following pairs of sentences by using otherwise. Follow the models given above.

1. Be more careful. If you aren't more careful, you'll burn your fingers.
2. I grabbed her hand. If I hadn't grabbed her hand, she would have slipped and fallen.
3. They must have gone out. If they weren't out, they would open the door.
4. Tom wants a higher salary. If he doesn't get a higher salary, he is going to resign.
5. Take an umbrella with you. If you don't take an umbrella, you might get wet.
6. We must save more money. If we don't save more money, we won't be able to take a vacation this year.
7. They had a map. If they hadn't had a map, they would have gotten lost.
8. Look out! If you don't look out, you'll get run over.
9. The children must have been tired. If they hadn't been tired, they wouldn't have gone to sleep so quickly.
10. You'll have to get more exercise. If you don't get more exercise, you'll get fat.

Mrs. Winters was tired after a day of shopping, so she went into a coffee shop to have some coffee and to rest for a few minutes before going back to the hotel where she and her husband were staying. While she was sitting at the counter sipping her coffee, she suddenly remembered that 5 she had to buy some cough medicine for her husband.

"Is there a drugstore near here?" she asked the man behind the counter.

"Yes, ma'am," the man said. "There's one about three blocks from here. Turn right when you go out the door, then 10 go to the second intersection and turn left. You'll see the drugstore at the end of the block on the right-hand side. It closes at five, but if you hurry, you'll get there in time."

Mrs. Winters followed the directions carefully and found the drugstore without any difficulty. She bought the cough 15 medicine and started to make her way back to the coffee shop. But after she had walked for about ten minutes and there was still no sign of the coffee shop, she realized that she must have made a mistake.

"Oh! I'm so dumb!" thought Mrs. Winters. "I left my 20 shopping bags in that coffee shop and now I'm lost."

She was still wondering what to do when a policeman came up to her and asked if he could help. Mrs. Winters explained what had happened.

"Well, first of all," said the policeman, "we'd better start with the drugstore you went to. Where was it?" Mrs. Winters held up the bag with the cough medicine in it so that the policeman could see the name of the store on the bag. 25

"Now," suggested the policeman, "we'll see if we can retrace your steps. Tell me again what directions they gave you at the restaurant." 30

After Mrs. Winters carefully repeated the instructions given to her by the man at the coffee shop, the policeman thought for a moment and then said, "Oh, you must have been at Harold's on Cornell Street! That's just two blocks from here. I'm going in that direction so I'll show you where it is." 35

A. *Choose the best answer.*
Mrs. Winters called herself "dumb" because
a. she had walked for ten minutes before she realized that she had gotten lost.
b. she could not find the drugstore.
c. she had left her shopping bags in a coffee shop which she could not find.
d. she had to ask a policeman for directions.

B. *Answer the following questions in your own words. Answer each question with a single complete sentence.*
1. Why had Mrs. Winters come to the city with her husband?
2. How far was the drugstore from the coffee shop?
3. When did Mrs. Winters realize that she had made a mistake?

C. *Answer these questions, using only short answers.*
1. Did the man behind the counter give Mrs. Winters good directions?
2. Did Mrs. Winters reach the drugstore in time?
3. Did the policeman go with Mrs. Winters as far as the drugstore?

D. Complete the following sentences. Your answers must be related to the ideas contained in the reading.

1. Mrs. Winters went to the coffee shop for a cup of coffee because _____ .
2. Mrs. Winters's husband had a bad cough, so _____ .
3. Mrs. Winters had to hurry to the drugstore because

   _____ .
4. The policeman came up to Mrs. Winters and asked her, "_____ ?"
5. Mrs. Winters might not have found the coffee shop again if _____ .

E. Choose the best explanation according to the story.

   in time (13) means
   a. eventually
   b. punctually
   c. before it closes
   d. at the right time

F. Find words or phrases in the reading which closely match the following phrases.

1. instructions how to get to a place
2. to return
3. coffee shop

G. Composition Imagine that you are the policeman mentioned in the reading. Describe what happened from the time you first saw Mrs. Winters until you showed her Harold's on Cornell Street. Do not introduce any ideas which are not included in the reading. Limit your composition to 90 words.

H. Turn the following sentences, which are in direct speech, into indirect speech. Follow the example:

   Mrs. Winters said, "I left my shopping bags in the coffee shop."
   Mrs. Winters said that she left her shopping bags in the coffee shop.

1. Mrs. Winters asked the man behind the counter, "Is there a drugstore near here?"
2. The man told her, "There's one about three blocks from here."

3. He told her, "Turn right when you go out the door."
4. He said, "You'll see the drugstore at the end of the block on the right-hand side."
5. He said that the drugstore closed at five, but, "If you hurry, you'll get there in time."
6. Mrs. Winters thought, "I'm so dumb!"
7. The policeman said, "First of all, we'd better start with the drugstore you went to."
8. The policeman suggested, "We'll see if we can retrace your steps."
9. The policeman said, "You must have been at Harold's on Cornell Street!"
10. The policeman took Mrs. Winters in the direction of Harold's and said, "I'll show you where it is."

As the train neared the resort town on the coast where I was going to spend my two-week vacation, I got up from my seat and wandered up the aisle to stretch my legs for a few minutes. At the front end of the car, I stopped and exchanged a few words with one of the passengers that I had met earlier in the station. He had bought me a cup of coffee then.

When I turned to go back to my seat, I happened to glance down the aisle and sitting just a few rows back was a man who had lived next door to me several years before. He was an incessant talker, I remembered, and it used to take hours to get away from him once he started a conversation. I was not at all sorry when he moved away from our neighborhood. We had not seen each other since then, and I certainly did not want to spoil my vacation by renewing an acquaintance with him now.

Luckily at that moment he was much too busy talking to the man next to him to catch sight of me. I slipped past him back to my seat, took down my two suitcases and carried them to the other end of the car so that I could be ready to get off the train as soon as it pulled into the station. The moment the train stopped, I got off and quickly made my way through the crowd to the line of taxis waiting in front of the station. As the taxi headed toward my motel at the north end of the beach, I breathed a deep sigh of relief at my narrow escape. There was little chance that I would run into my boring ex-neighbor again.

When I reached the motel, I registered and went straight to my room. Since I was going to be there for two full weeks, I decided to unpack my things and get settled before going out to eat. As soon as I had emptied the suitcases, I left my room and headed for the restaurant across the street. I had barely stepped through the door of the restaurant when an all too familiar voice greeted me. I had not escaped from my tiresome next-door neighbor after all! He grasped me warmly by the hand and insisted that we have dinner together.

"This *is* a pleasant surprise," he said. "I never expected to see you again after all these years."

A. Choose the best answer.

This is a story about a man who

a. got off the train to avoid meeting an ex-neighbor.
b. went with an ex-neighbor to spend a weekend at the beach.
c. tried to get away from an ex-neighbor but did not succeed.
d. was surprised to meet his ex-neighbor in a small motel on the coast.

B. Answer the following questions in your own words. Answer each question with a single complete sentence.

1. Why did the writer want to avoid his ex-neighbor?
2. Why did the writer feel sure that he had escaped from his ex-neighbor?
3. What was the writer doing when his ex-neighbor greeted him?

C. Answer these questions, using only short answers.

1. Did the writer speak to anyone in the aisle?
2. Did it take the writer long to get out of the station?
3. Did the writer recognize his ex-neighbor's voice at once?

D. Complete the following sentences. Your answers must be related to the ideas contained in the reading.

1. The writer had not seen his ex-neighbor since _____ .
2. The writer got back to his seat without being seen because _____ .
3. When the train stopped, the writer _____ and made his way through the crowd to _____ .
4. The motel was located _____ .
5. "We must _____ ," said the ex-neighbor, grasping _____ .

E. Choose the best explanation according to the story.

boring (26) means

a. weary
b. tiresome
c. talkative
d. sleepy

44

F. Find words or phrases in the reading which closely match the following phrases.

1. ceaseless, nonstop
2. returned without being noticed
3. nearly unsuccessful flight

G. Composition Describe what the writer did from the time he went back to his seat until his ex-neighbor greeted him in the restaurant. Do not introduce any ideas which are not included in the reading. Limit your composition to 90 words.

H. Look at this sentence:

He had bought *me a cup of coffee* then.

The indirect object *(me)* precedes the direct object *(a cup of coffee)*, when the indirect object is shorter, and therefore less emphasized, than the direct object. Compare these two sentences:

I lent *him my book*.
I lent *my book to the student* who sits in front of me.

Now complete the following sentences by arranging the two objects (in parentheses) according to the length and degree of emphasis necessary. For example:

I paid _____ *(the man) (the money)*.
I paid the man the money.
She wrote _____ *(the principal of her son's school) (a letter)*.
She wrote a letter to the principal of her son's school.

1. I've just been out buying _____ *(a friend of mine who is getting married) (a wedding present)*.
2. She made _____ *(me) (a hot cup of coffee)*.
3. He gave _____ *(his niece) (all the money he had in his pocket)*.
4. They are going to give _____ *(the students with the highest scores on the test) (certificates)*.
5. Nobody has sent _____ *(me) (any Christmas cards)* yet.
6. I had to show _____ *(the guard at the building entrance) (my pass)* before I was allowed in.

7. I sent _____ *(the editor of the* Chicago Times*) (my article).*

8. He showed _____ *(us all) (a photograph of his oldest daughter).*

9. John has never bought _____ *(his wife) (a bouquet of flowers).*

10. She always makes _____ *(anyone who visits her) (coffee).*

"You do buy old books, don't you?" asked Fred, putting his box down on the counter.

"I'll have to see what you have before I can answer that question," the man behind the counter said. "Business isn't as good as it used to be. People don't seem to be very interested in collecting rare books anymore." 5

Fred opened his box and laid the books out on the counter.

"I don't pretend to know much about old books," he said. "I've had these for years, and I haven't even read them. My grandfather left them to me, as a matter of fact. But my wife 10 is always after me to get rid of them. She says they are just cluttering up our apartment. So I thought I'd bring them in to show them to you, just in case they happened to be worth something."

In the meantime, the man was picking up the books one 15 by one and examining them. He shook his head.

"They're not worth very much," he said. "I can give you three or four dollars for them if you want to get rid of them. I can't offer you much more, I'm afraid."

When he picked up the last book, however, his expression 20 changed and his eyes lighted up all of a sudden.

"What is it?" asked Fred.

"Now this one *is* worth something!" exclaimed the man, turning the pages carefully. "It's a very rare edition."

He handed the book to Fred, who looked at the title. It was 25 a novel by an author that he had never heard of. Of all the books he had packed up to bring in, this one had looked the least interesting.

"How much is it worth?" he asked.

"How much?" the man repeated. "I can't tell you exactly. 30 But not less than four hundred dollars, I would say. I'm only guessing, of course. It might be worth a little more than that."

It was Fred's turn to be excited. He thought of what he could do with four hundred dollars, and he wondered what 35 his wife would say now about his having "cluttered up" their apartment with old books.

A. Choose the best answer.

Fred took the old books to the bookseller because
a. he never had time to read them.
b. his wife did not like having them in the house.
c. he wanted to find out what they were worth.
d. he expected to make a lot of money with them.

B. Answer the following questions in your own words. Answer each question with a single complete sentence.

1. How much did the bookseller offer Fred for the first books?
2. Why was the last book worth a lot of money?
3. How much did the bookseller think that the last book might be worth?

C. Answer these questions, using only short answers.

1. Did the bookseller find it easy to sell old books?
2. Did the bookseller examine all the books?
3. Did Fred expect the last book to be worth a lot of money?

D. Complete the following sentences. Your answers must be related to the ideas contained in the reading.

1. As he put his box down on the counter, Fred asked the bookseller whether _____ .
2. Fred laid the books out on the counter so that

   _____ .
3. Fred had had the books for years, although _____ .
4. Fred _____ , but the bookseller couldn't tell him exactly.
5. Fred was excited at the thought of _____ .

E. Choose the best explanation according to the story.

cluttering up our apartment (12) means
a. stacked to the ceiling
b. causing higher rent
c. making the apartment less roomy
d. making the apartment look messy

F. Find words or phrases in the reading which closely match the following phrases.

1. urging me
2. became bright
3. very limited in number

G. Composition   Imagine that you are Fred. Describe what happened from the time the bookseller first began to examine the books until he told you how much the last book might be worth. Do not introduce any ideas which are not included in the reading. Limit your composition to 90 words.

H. Look at this sentence:

Business isn't as good as it *used to* be.

Here *used to* describes a state of affairs which lasted for some time in the past, but has since changed. *Used to* can also indicate habits which have been given up. Here are some more examples of its use:

I don't smoke as much as I *used to*.

He *used to* go to work by train.

Mary *didn't use to* have such long hair.

Using the verb list below, complete the following sentences with use(d) to + verb (main form).

bark	enjoy	sit
be	live	spend
belong to	ring	take
cost		

1. Our neighbor John had a dog that _____ all night.
2. The bell _____ at the end of every class.
3. As soon as he received any money, he _____ it.
4. That's the cabin where Abe Lincoln _____.
5. When we were children, it _____ us an hour to walk home from school.
6. On summer evenings we _____ in the yard after dinner.
7. He eats too much. He _____ so fat. (*Use the negative.*)

8. I _____ reading the letters you wrote me when you were overseas.
9. Eggs are expensive right now, but I can remember when they _____ a penny apiece.
10. The books that Fred sold _____ his grandfather.

It was a quarter after nine as Marie hurried into the office
building where she was going to work. Her bus had inched
along through heavy morning traffic, making her a few
minutes late for her very first job. She resolved to start out
half an hour earlier the next day.   5

Once inside the lobby, she had to stand at the elevators
and wait several minutes before she could get on one going
to the sixth floor. When she finally reached the office
marked "King Enterprises," she knocked on the door
nervously and waited. There was no answer. She tapped on   10
the door again, but still there was no reply. From inside the
next office, she could hear the sound of voices, so she opened
the door and went in.

Although she was sure it was the same office she had been
in two weeks before when she had had the interview with   15
Mr. King, it looked quite different now. In fact, it hardly
looked like an office at all. The employees were just standing
around chatting and smoking. At the far end of the room,
somebody must have just told a good joke, she concluded,
because there was a loud burst of laughter as she came in.   20
For a moment she had thought they were laughing at her.

Then one of the men looked at his watch, clapped his
hands and said something to the others. Quickly they all

went to their desks and, in a matter of seconds, everyone
was hard at work. No one paid any attention to Marie.   25
Finally she went up to the man who was sitting at the desk
nearest the door and explained that this was her first day in
the office. Hardly looking up from his work, he told her to
have a seat and wait for Mr. King, who would arrive at any
moment. Then Marie realized that the day's work in the   30
office began just before Mr. King arrived. Later she found
out that he lived in Connecticut and came into Manhattan
on the same train every morning, arriving in the office
promptly at 9:35, so that his staff knew exactly when to start
working.   35

A. Choose the best answer.

Marie hardly recognized the office she went into because
a. she had been there only once before.
b. people were making so much noise in the office.
c. she was still feeling very nervous.
d. nobody was doing any work.

B. Answer the following questions in your own words. Answer each question with a single complete sentence.

1. Why had the bus made Marie late?
2. How did Marie get to the sixth floor?
3. Whose voices could Marie hear from the next office?

C. Answer these questions, using only short answers.

1. Was Mr. King in his office when Marie knocked on the door?
2. Were the people in the office laughing at Marie?
3. Did Mr. King live in the city?

D. Complete the following sentences. Your answers must be related to the ideas contained in the reading.

1. Marie resolved to leave home earlier the next day in order to _____.
2. The office Marie was going to work in was on the sixth floor, so _____.
3. It hardly looked like an office that morning because _____.

4. When one of the men clapped his hands, he must have said, "_____."

5. Marie had to wait for Mr. King because _____ .

E. Choose the best explanation according to the story.

resolved (4) means

a. found a solution

b. thought about

c. agreed

d. was determined

F. Find words or phrases in the reading which closely match the following words and phrases.

1. went very slowly

2. answer

3. exactly

G. Composition   Imagine that you are Marie. Describe what you did and saw from the time you entered the office until the man told you to sit down. Do not introduce any ideas which are not included in the reading. Limit your composition to 90 words.

H. Look at this sentence:

Somebody *must have* just *told* a good joke, because there was a loud burst of laughter.

Must + Present Perfect (*have* + past participle) indicates a very probable conclusion drawn from a given situation. In this case, it is probable — almost certain — that the man had told a very funny joke because everyone laughed loudly.

Now complete these sentences using *must* + *Present Perfect* (*have* + *past participle*).

1. The streets are wet. It _____ *(rain)* last night.

2. I didn't hear anything. I _____ *(be)* asleep.

3. Marie got the job. She _____ *(make)* a good impression.

4. John promised to call. I wonder why he hasn't. He _____ *(forget)* .

5. Someone _____ (leave) the cage door open. The bird has gotten out.
6. That's a lovely dress you're wearing. It _____ (cost) a lot of money.
7. Mr. King is late this morning. He _____ (miss) his train.
8. You look pleased. You _____ (have) some good news.
9. I know how this book is going to end. I _____ (read) it before.
10. You _____ (make) a mistake. Mr. Brown doesn't live here anymore.

It was dark in the attic, just as Miss Lee had warned him.
Jim found the small end windows and forced them open,
letting in more light. He could just make out the boxes
which Miss Lee had told him about.

"When my father died," Miss Lee had said, "his large   5
library was donated to the University. Most of his papers
and some other possessions of no great value were stored in
boxes and put up in the attic. They've been there ever since.
I don't suppose anyone has gone in there for over ten years."

"What about his diaries?" asked Jim. "In one of his letters   10
to a colleague, Dr. Lee mentioned that he kept a diary."

"I don't remember seeing any diaries," said Miss Lee, with
a puzzled look on her face. "Of course, he may have
destroyed them before his last illness. Otherwise, they must
be in one of those boxes in the attic."   15

"I see," said Jim. "In that case, would you permit me to go
through those boxes? If I can find the diaries, I'll probably be
able to write a much more complete account of your father's
life."

"Certainly," said Miss Lee. "You can't imagine how   20
pleased I am that you've taken an interest in writing a book
about my father. I would have taken better care of his papers
if I had known."

After searching through a number of drawers, Miss Lee
found the key to the attic.   25

"It may not be light enough to see anything up there," she
said as she handed him the key. "There are small windows
at each end of the attic, but I suspect they'll be covered with
dust and won't let much light in."

There were about a dozen boxes in all. Jim did not know   30
where to begin. He opened first one, then the other, but did
not find anything that looked like a diary. Then he decided
to try the largest box. It was full of papers. As he began to
sort through stacks of papers, a bundle of note pads tied
together with string caught his eye. On the cover of the top   35
one were scribbled the words, "Diary—1946-47."

A. Choose the best answer.

Jim wanted to find Dr. Lee's diaries because
a. he was interested in the professor's private life.
b. they were mentioned in one of the professor's letters.
c. he thought that the professor's daughter was not taking good enough care of her father's papers.
d. he wanted to write as complete as possible an account of the professor's life.

B. Answer the following questions in your own words. Use one complete sentence for each answer.

1. Why was it dark in the attic?
2. When were the boxes put up in the attic?
3. Who was Jim?

C. Answer these questions, using only short answers.

1. Were Dr. Lee's books also put up in the attic?
2. Did Miss Lee give Jim permission to look in the boxes?
3. Did Miss Lee find the key to the attic easily?

D. Complete the following sentences. Your answers must be related to the ideas contained in the reading.

1. There was more light in the attic after _____ .
2. Miss Lee looked puzzled when Jim _____ .
3. Miss Lee thought that _____ before his last illness.
4. Jim wanted to go through all the boxes in order to

   _____ .

5. When Jim opened the largest box, he found that

   _____ .

E. Choose the best explanation according to the story.

scribbled (36) means
a. written sloppily
b. spoken
c. written carefully
d. printed

F. Find words or phrases in the reading which closely match the following phrases.

1. see with difficulty
2. not worth very much
3. attracted his attention

G. Composition　　Imagine that you are Miss Lee. Write a
letter to your sister, telling her about Jim's visit and
how he discovered the diaries. Include appropriate
details from the passage. Use your own words as much
as possible. Limit your composition to 100 words.

H. Look at this sentence:
　　He *may have destroyed* them before his last illness.
May + Present Perfect (*have* + past participle) indicates
a possibility—usually in the past—which we are
uncertain about. In this case, Miss Lee is not certain
whether her father destroyed the diaries or not.

　Now complete the following sentences by using may +
Present Perfect of the verbs given in parentheses.

1. I _____ *(tell)* you this story before. Stop me if I
   have.
2. If the book isn't on the shelf, someone _____
   (borrow) it.
3. The man who lives in that house is an artist by the
   name of Long. You _____ *(hear)* of him.
4. Let's go out in about half an hour. The rain _____
   (stop) by then.
5. I can't remember what happened to the picture. It
   _____ *(be given away)*.
6. She seemed to be telling the truth but, for all I know,
   she _____ *(tell)* me a lie.
7. After that, we don't know what Smith did. He
   _____ *(stay)* at home, as he said, or he _____
   (go out).
8. Then I heard something moving under the bed. Of
   course it _____ *(be)* only a mouse.
9. If he isn't on this plane, he _____ *(decided)* not to
   come after all.
10. The man _____ *(be called)* Robinson. I really don't
    remember.

21 Beacon Road
Stockton, Maine
November 7, 1978

Dear Mr. Fenton:

On December 1st we are planning to have a dinner to   5
celebrate the fifth anniversary of the Stockton Clean
Environment Agency and I have been asked by our
committee to invite you to be the guest of honor on this
occasion. Since you came to live in our community last year,
you have always shown a great deal of interest in our   10
activities and you are without doubt our most popular
speaker. We shall all be delighted as well as honored if you
can once again find the time to spend an evening with us. I
will send you further details as soon as I hear from you. I
hope you will be able to accept this invitation.   15

Sincerely,
Joan Edwards
Secretary
Stockton Clean Environment Agency

Riverside Apartments   20
Stockton, Maine
November 12, 1978

Dear Ms. Edwards:

Thank you for your letter of November 7th, which I am
answering on behalf of my husband. Apparently you have   25
not heard that about a month ago my husband was taken
seriously ill. Although he is much better now, the doctor has
ordered him to take a complete rest for at least three
months. As a matter of fact, we are leaving for Hawaii just
as soon as he is able to travel and we will probably not   30
return until after the middle of February.

In view of this, I regret that my husband is unable to
accept your kind invitation to the dinner which you are
having on December 1st. He has asked me, however, to send
his best wishes and congratulations to you on your fifth   35

anniversary, and to say that he hopes to see you again in the spring.

Sincerely,
Sylvia Fenton

A. *Choose the best answer.*

Mrs. Fenton refused the invitation on behalf of her husband because

a. he was seriously ill.
b. he was recovering from a serious illness.
c. he was going on vacation to Hawaii.
d. the doctor had ordered him to stay in bed for three months.

B. *Answer the following questions in your own words. Use one complete sentence for each answer.*

1. When was the Stockton Clean Environment Agency founded?
2. Why was Mr. Fenton asked to be the guest of honor?
3. How long had Mr. Fenton been sick?

C. *Answer these questions, using only short answers.*

1. Had Mr. Fenton lived in Stockton for a long time?
2. Had Mr. Fenton attended previous meetings of the Stockton Clean Environment Agency?
3. Did the Fentons intend to stay in Stockton that winter?

D. *Complete the following sentences. Your answers must be related to the ideas contained in the reading.*

1. The Stockton Clean Environment Agency was planning to have a dinner on December 1st because _____.
2. Ms. Edwards promised to send further details of the dinner as soon as _____.
3. Mrs. Fenton answered Ms. Edwards's letter on behalf of her husband because _____.
4. "Your husband _____," the doctor told Mrs. Fenton.
5. If Mr. Fenton had not been taken ill, he _____.

E. Choose the best explanation according to the story.

hear from (14) means
a. listen to
b. understand the reasons
c. get a letter from
d. get a message from

F. Find words or phrases in the letters which closely match the following phrases.

1. liked by everyone
2. additional
3. it seems (that)

G. Composition
Imagine that you are Ms. Edwards. Write a letter to Mrs. Fenton which conveys your sympathy on learning of her husband's illness. Limit your letter to 75 words.

H. Look at these sentences:

I *hope* you will be able to accept this invitation.

I *regret* that my husband is unable to accept.

There are a number of verbs in English, such as *see, hear, like, know, understand, remember, believe (think)*, etc., which are rarely found in the continuous form (*be +* verb-*ing*). These are verbs of perception or verbs which express a mental state or condition.

Here are some more examples:

I *like* Mary's new dress.

John *doesn't understand* what you are saying.

They *want* to stay home.

Other common verbs used in this way are: *seem, look (seem), belong to, contain, matter, mean.*

Now complete the following sentences by using the correct form of the verb (Simple Present or Present Continuous).

1. I _____ *(know)* I've seen that movie, but I _____ *(not, remember)* what it's about.
2. I _____ *(think)* she _____ *(wash)* her hair.
3. _____ you _____ *(know)* what this word _____ *(mean)*?

4. I _____ *(see)* you are busy. What _____ you
   _____ *(do)*?
5. That policeman _____ *(look)* as if he _____
   (want) us to stop.
6. I _____ *(think)* someone _____ *(knock)* on the
   door.
7. That coat she _____ *(wear)* today _____
   (belong to) her sister.
8. I _____ *(hope)* those children _____ *(know)*
   how to swim.
9. _____ anyone _____ *(know)* what this envelope
   _____ *(contain)*?
10. It _____ *(not, matter)* if they _____ *(not, like)*
    it.

A small crowd had gathered near the entrance to the park. His curiosity aroused, Jeff crossed the street to see what was happening. He found that the center of attraction was an old man with a performing monkey. He soon discovered that the monkey's tricks were not spectacular so, after throwing a few coins into the hat which the man had placed on the sidewalk, Jeff began to move away, along with other members of the crowd. 5

At this point the man suddenly let out a loud cry. Everyone turned to see what had happened. The man was bending over his monkey, which now was lying stretched out on the sidewalk. He picked up the lifeless body and, holding it close to him, began to cry. A young man stepped forward from the crowd, took out his wallet and dropped several dollar bills into the hat. Jeff and several other people followed the young man's example, and soon the hat was filled with coins and dollar bills. Meanwhile the man continued to hold the dead monkey in his arms and seemed to be oblivious to what was going on around him. 10

A few months later, Jeff came across the old man again in another part of the city. The man had a monkey, bought no doubt with the money which the crowd had given him, but the new monkey did not seem to be any better at its tricks than the previous one. Jeff was pleased to see that the old man was still able to earn a living, though this time, having partly paid for the monkey out of his own pocket, he did not feel obliged to throw any money into the hat. 20

But the performance was not over yet! Once again the old man let out a loud cry. And once again the monkey was suddenly lying motionless on the sidewalk. The man picked up the "dead" monkey and, clutching it in his arms, began to cry. The same young man stepped forward and threw some money into the hat. Again the crowd responded—but not Jeff. Smiling to himself, he went on his way, amazed at the man's ingenuity. 30

35

A. *Choose the best answer.*
Jeff did not throw any money into the hat the second time because

a. there was enough money in it already.
b. he had seen the monkey's tricks before.
c. the monkey's tricks were not very good.
d. he knew that the monkey was not really dead.

**B. Answer the following questions in your own words. Use
one complete sentence for each answer.**
1. What was the crowd doing near the entrance to the park?
2. Why did the crowd soon begin to move away?
3. What was the old man doing while the crowd threw money into his hat?

C. Answer these questions, using only short answers.
1. Did the people throw a lot of money into the hat when they thought that the monkey was dead?
2. Was there much money in the hat already?
3. Did the old man thank the crowd for throwing money into his hat?

**D. Complete the following sentences. Your answers must
be related to the ideas contained in the reading.**
1. _____ for people to throw money in.
2. The old man let out a loud cry in order to _____.
3. It was a young man who first _____ and _____.
   Then Jeff and the others did likewise.
4. Jeff thought that _____ with the money which the crowd had given him.
5. Jeff didn't think that the new monkey's tricks
   _____.

E. Choose the best explanation according to the story.
spectacular (5) means
a. dramatic and
   interesting
b. easy to see
c. illusory
d. inventive and varied

**F. Find words or phrases in the reading which closely
match the following phrases.**
1. without movement

2. holding tightly
3. cleverness

G. Composition   Imagine that you are Jeff. Write a letter
to a friend explaining the trick which the old man
played on the crowd. Use your own words as much as
possible. Limit your letter to 100 words.

H. Look at this sentence:
The man *continued to hold* the dead monkey in his
arms.

In this pattern, the verb *continue* is followed by *to* + the
main form of the verb *hold*.
Does she *want to go* to bed early?
They were *trying* hard *not to laugh*.
Compare this with the pattern where the verb is
followed by a gerund (see Exercise G on page 14):
The children *enjoy playing* in the park.

*Now complete the sentences below by using the correct
form of a verb from the list.*

become	help	tell
buy	invite	travel
finish	turn off	understand
smoke		

1. Don't forget _____ the light before you go to bed.
2. We are not allowed _____ in the classroom.
3. The man refused _____ the policeman his name
   and address.
4. You promised _____ me a newspaper when you
   went shopping.
5. Mary wants _____ either a nurse or a social
   worker when she gets out of school.
6. When I spoke to him in English, he pretended not
   _____ what I was saying.
7. Tom hopes _____ writing his letters by four
   o'clock.
8. Even when I have a lot of work to do, you never offer
   _____ me.
9. In the end, they decided not _____ by ship.
10. I meant _____ you to the party, but I forgot.

"Now," said Detective Travis, pulling up a chair close to the injured man's bed and sitting down. "I hope you feel well enough to answer a few questions."

"Yes, I guess so," said the man lying in the bed. He tried to raise himself up slightly, but the effort seemed too much for 5 him. The nurse placed another pillow behind his head and left the room. "I'll be back in just a few minutes," she told the detective.

"First of all," said the detective, opening his memo pad, "we have to establish your identity." 10

The man looked astonished. "My identity . . . ," he said slowly. "Don't you even know who I am? How long have I been lying here like this?"

"Three days," the detective told him. "But we found no identification of any kind on you. Whoever beat you up also 15 stole your wallet."

"Whoever beat me up . . .?" echoed the man. "I don't remember anybody beating me up . . . ."

"You were attacked by someone and your car was stolen too," the detective explained patiently. "So you see, we've 20 been completely in the dark. We haven't had much to work on. You were found Tuesday night lying unconscious in a parking lot behind the New Moon Restaurant, where you had stopped for dinner that evening. That's all we know about you. Anyway, maybe now you can tell us who you are 25 and what happened to you last Tuesday night."

The man raised his right hand to his bandaged head and said slowly, "I . . . I'm not sure . . . what happened . . ."

"We think somebody attacked you when you were getting in your car," the detective continued. "They were probably 30 watching you when you came out of the restaurant. Then when you unlocked your car and started to get in, they sneaked up behind you. You received a very heavy blow on the head. Can't you remember anything that happened?"

Closing his eyes, the injured man sighed deeply and 35 murmured, "No . . . I don't remember what happened . . . I . . . I remember . . ."

The detective nodded and waited for him to go on.

". . . it was raining and . . . I was getting soaked . . . ," the

man continued. "Somebody . . . two men . . . put me in a car, 40
but . . . it wasn't a car . . . it was a big van . . . ."

"An ambulance," the detective said, interrupting him.
"That was after the owner of the restaurant found you in the
parking lot. He called an ambulance. It was pouring down
rain. But what happened before that?" 45

"I don't know . . . ." the man replied. "I can't remember
anything else!"

"Who are you?" the detective asked. "What's your name
and where do you live?"

"I . . . I don't know . . . ," the man murmured. "I . . . don't 50
remember . . . ." His words were trailing away and he was
breathing deeply now. The detective looked up at the nurse
who had come back into the room and was standing beside
the bed.

"It's no use," the nurse told the detective. "He can't hear 55
you. You'll have to come back tomorrow."

Stuffing his memo pad back in his pocket, the detective
said, "I'm afraid we have an amnesia victim on our hands."

A. Choose the best answer.

The detective did not know who the man was because
a. they had not caught the man who attacked him.
b. his car had been stolen.
c. both his car and his wallet had been stolen.
d. he had been unconscious.

B. Answer the following questions in your own words. Use one complete sentence for each answer.

1. Why did the victim look astonished?
2. Where was the victim attacked?
3. What may the victim have been doing when he was attacked?

C. Answer these questions, using only short answers.

1. Was the victim willing to answer the detective's questions?
2. Was the nurse present while the detective questioned the victim?
3. Did the victim know his name and address?

D. Complete the following sentences. Your answers must be related to the ideas contained in the reading.

1. Detective Travis sat down on the chair which he
   _____ .

2. The victim could not raise himself up, so the nurse
   _____ .

3. If the victim's wallet had not been stolen, the police
   _____ .

4. "As you were getting into your car, we think your
   attacker _____ ."

5. "_____ ," said the restaurant owner on the phone.

E. Choose the best explanation according to the passage.
in the dark (21) means
a. at night
b. obscure
c. hidden
d. not knowing anything

F. Find words or phrases in the reading which closely match the following phrases.
1. bringing near to
2. make certain who a person is
3. surprised

G. Composition Imagine that you are Detective Travis.
Write a short report of what occurred while you were
with the victim. Use your own words as much as
possible. Limit your report to 90 words.

H. Look at these sentences:

You have been lying here *since* Tuesday night.
You have been lying here *for* three days.
Since is used to indicate the point of time at which the
action or event began.

	last week.
I have known him *since*	April.
	I came to live in this town.

For is used to indicate the period of time over which an
action or event has lasted.

	ten minutes.
She has been waiting *for*	about half an hour.
	more than a week.

***Now write each of the following sentences twice, using
either* for *or* since *with the expressions of time given in
parentheses.***

1. The detective has been in the victim's room _____
   (about an hour) (the nurse came out).
2. That man has been standing at the corner _____
   (two o'clock) (ages).
3. They've been married _____ *(last Easter) (just
   eight months)*.
4. It hasn't stopped raining _____ *(over twelve
   hours) (last night)*.
5. We've been sailing now _____ *(three weeks)
   (August 15th)*.
6. I've been reading *War and Peace* _____
   (Christmas) (the last two months).
7. Mr. Brown hasn't spoken to his next-door neighbor
   _____ *(twenty years) (1955)*.
8. John has been working in this office _____ *(he
   graduated from high school) (nearly eighteen
   months)*.
9. No one has lived in this house _____ *(1875) (over
   a century)*.
10. The mailman hasn't brought me a letter _____
    (last week) (the last week).

We first became aware that something unusual was happening when one of the ship's officers came up to the Chief Engineer who was sitting at our table, and spoke to him in a low voice. The Chief Engineer got up from the table immediately and with a brief excuse, which told us nothing,   5 left the dining room. At first we thought that there had been an accident or that a fire had broken out on board, but in a few minutes word went around that a man had been seen floating in the ocean. We noticed that the ship was slowing down, and then, with a sudden violent motion, it began to   10 turn around. Some of the passengers did not wait to finish their meal but immediately rushed up on deck. Others crowded around the portholes. There was so much confusion in the dining room that we finally decided to join those who had gone up on deck.   15

Once we stepped out on deck, we found out that one of the crew had seen a man in the ocean some distance from the ship. He had informed the captain, and the captain had ordered the ship to be turned around at once. We were now only about two hundred yards or so from the man, and a   20 lifeboat had already been lowered into the water. In it there were four crewmembers, an officer and the ship's doctor. The officer shouted an order and the crew began to row away

from the ship. Looking in the direction the lifeboat was
heading, we were able to make out the exact position of the   25
man in the water. He was holding on to some large object
that might have been a broken section of a small fishing
boat.

The lifeboat finally reached the man and two of the
crewmembers managed to hoist the man into the boat.   30

Then the crew began to row back to the ship again. The
rescued man, wrapped in a blanket, was helped up the rope
ladder and onto the deck. Leaning on the arm of the ship's
doctor, but still able to walk in spite of his experience, he
was led off to the ship's hospital. As they passed along the   35
deck, everyone cheered and applauded.

A. Choose the best answer.
The people at the writer's table decided to leave the
dining room because
a. the ship was turning around quite violently.
b. the Chief Engineer had already left.
c. a man had been seen floating in the ocean.
d. they could not continue their meal in peace.

**B. Answer the following questions in your own words. Use
one complete sentence for each answer.**
1. Why did some of the passengers crowd around the
portholes?
2. How were the people on deck able to make out where
the man in the water was?
3. How did the man in the water manage to stay afloat?

C. Answer these questions, using only short answers.
1. Could the writer and his friends hear what the officer
said to the Chief Engineer?
2. Had the lifeboat already been lowered into the sea by
the time the writer and his friends came up on deck?
3. Was the rescued man carried to the ship's hospital?

**D. Complete the following sentences. Your answers must
be related to the ideas contained in the reading.**
1. Some of the passengers rushed up on deck before
——————.

2. The writer and his friends left their table because
   _____.

3. The captain ordered the ship to be turned around so
   that _____.

4. The sailors in the lifeboat began to row as soon as
   _____.

5. Even though the rescued man had had a rough
   experience, _____.

E. *Choose the best explanation according to the story.*
   became aware (1) means
   a. were frightened
   b. knew
   c. imagined
   d. decided

F. *Find words or phrases in the passage which closely*
   match the following phrases.
   1. people began to tell one another
   2. disorder
   3. a long way

G. *Composition*   Imagine that you are the man in the
   ocean. Describe what happened from the time you saw
   the ship begin to slow down until you were taken
   aboard. Do not introduce any ideas which are not in the
   reading. Use your own words as much as possible. Limit
   your story to 100 words.

H. *In the reading there are several examples of the use of*
   the Passive (be + past participle). Study these and then
   complete the following sentences by putting the verb in
   parentheses into an appropriate tense in the Passive.
   1. The man who _____ *(rescue)* had been in the
      ocean for ten hours.
   2. It always rains when the windows _____ just
      _____ *(wash)*.
   3. The thief _____ last _____ *(see)* wearing a blue
      suit.
   4. I don't think the letter will arrive in time unless it
      _____ *(send)* by air.

71

5. It won't be safe to use these stairs until they
   _____ (repair).
6. Make sure the door _____ (lock) before you go to
   bed.
7. You _____ (stop) by a policeman if you try to cross
   the street now.
8. They wouldn't have gotten sick if the water _____
   (boil).
9. The grass looks as if it _____ (not, cut) for years.
10. His book fell into the river and _____ (lose)
    forever.

I left my friend's house shortly after six o'clock. It was still too early for dinner, I thought, so I walked along Beach Drive for about an hour until I began to feel hungry. By that time I was not far from a favorite restaurant of mine where I often went to have seafood. I knew the owner very well and had been going there for years.

I went into the restaurant, which was already crowded, and ordered a large bowl of clam chowder and my favorite seafood platter. While I was waiting for the chowder to arrive, I looked around the restaurant to see if there was anyone I knew. It was then that I noticed that a man sitting at a corner table near the door kept glancing in my direction, as if he knew me. I certainly did not know him, however. The man had a newspaper open in front of him, which he was pretending to read, but I could see that he was keeping an eye on me. When the waiter brought my clam chowder, the man was clearly puzzled by the familiar way in which the waiter and I chatted with each other. He seemed even more puzzled as time went on and it became obvious that all of the waiters in the restaurant knew me. Eventually he got up and went into the kitchen. After a few minutes he came out again, paid his bill and left without another glance in my direction.

When I had finished and was about to pay my bill, I called the owner of the restaurant and asked what the man had wanted. The owner seemed a little embarrassed by my question and at first did not want to tell me. I insisted. "Well," he said, "that man was a detective." "Really?" I said, showing my surprise. "He was certainly very interested in me. But why?" "He followed you here because he thought you were the man he was looking for," the owner of the restaurant said. "When he came into the kitchen, he showed me a photograph of the wanted man. I must say he looked very much like you! Of course, since we know you here, I was able to convince him that he had made a mistake." "It's lucky I came to a restaurant where I'm known," I said. "Otherwise, I might have been arrested."

A. Choose the best answer.

The man at the corner table kept looking at the writer because

a. he was bored with reading his newspaper.
b. he thought that the writer was someone wanted by the police.
c. he was afraid that the writer might run away.
d. he thought he recognized the writer.

B. Answer the following questions in your own words. Use one complete sentence for each answer.

1. About what time did the writer go to the restaurant?
2. What kind of food was served at that restaurant?
3. Why did the man at the corner table believe that the writer was the man he was after?

C. Answer these questions, using only short answers.

1. Did the detective look at the writer after he came out of the kitchen?
2. Had the writer already paid his bill when he called over the owner of the restaurant?
3. Was the detective following the wrong man?

D. Complete the following sentences. Your answers must be related to the ideas contained in the reading.

1. The writer walked along Beach Drive for about an hour because _____.
2. The detective was puzzled by the fact that _____.
3. The writer insisted that the restaurant owner tell him _____.
4. The detective _____, which he showed to the owner of the restaurant.
5. The detective didn't arrest the writer because

_____.

E. Choose the best explanation according to the story.

keeping an eye on (15) means

a. watching
b. looking at
c. glancing at
d. looking in the direction of

F. **Find words or phrases in the reading which closely match the following phrases.**

1. taking a quick look
2. bewildered
3. completely clear

G. **Composition**   Imagine that you are the detective. Describe what happened from the time you followed the man into the restaurant until you paid your bill and left. Do not introduce any ideas which are not in the reading. Use your own words as much as possible. Limit your composition to 90 words.

H. **Look at this sentence:**

The man *had* a newspaper *open* in front of him.

In the pattern verb + direct object + adjective, the adjective follows the object of the verb. Used in this way, the adjective frequently indicates a condition caused by the verbal action.

Here is another example:

She opened the cage door and *set* the bird *free*.

Now complete each sentence below by using an appropriate verb + adjective from the list.

break/open	make/clear	paint/red
find/empty	make/sick	keep/open
keep/warm	make/tired	get/clean
like/sweet	open/wide	

1. He spoke slowly and emphatically in order to _____ himself _____ .
2. When I opened my suitcase, I _____ it _____ . I'd been robbed!
3. Don't _____ your eyes _____ by reading in the dark.
4. Three spoons of sugar? You _____ your coffee _____ !
5. Why did they _____ the door _____ ? I liked the old color better.
6. You'll _____ yourself _____ if you eat all that candy.

7. She has six blankets on her bed in the winter, but she still can't _____ herself _____ .
8. We've used lots of soap and hot water, but we still haven't managed to _____ the sheets _____ .
9. You might have to _____ the drawer _____ . I think I've lost the key.
10. When the dentist tells me to _____ my mouth _____ , I always _____ my eyes _____ too!

One summer evening I was sitting by the open window, reading a good science fiction book. I was so engrossed in the story I was reading that I did not notice that it was getting dark. When I realized it was too dark for me to read easily, I put the book down and got up to turn on a light. Just as I was about to close the drapes, I heard someone crying, "Help! Help!" It seemed to come from the trees at the other end of the yard. I looked out but it was now too dark to see anything clearly. Almost immediately I heard the cry again. It sounded like a child, but I could not imagine what anybody would be doing in our backyard, unless one of the neighborhood children had climbed a tree and had not been able to get down.

I decided that I ought to go out and have a look in the yard, just in case someone was in trouble. I got a flashlight from the hall closet and picked up my son's baseball bat which was lying on the closet floor. I thought it might come in handy. Armed with these, I went out into the yard. Once again I heard the cry, and this time there was no doubt that it came from the trees at the far end of the yard. "Who's there?" I called out as I walked across the yard toward the trees. But there was no answer. With the help of my flashlight, I searched all over that end of the yard, including the branches of the trees. There was no sign of anybody or anything. I came to the conclusion that my imagination was playing tricks on me, probably because of the story I was reading about weird creatures on another planet.

Feeling rather foolish about stalking around in my own backyard with a baseball bat, I went back into the house and put the bat and the flashlight away. I had just sat down to read my book again when I was startled by the cry of "Help! Help!" this time from right behind me. I dropped my book and jumped up. There, sitting on the mantle over the fireplace, was a large green and red bird. It was my neighbor's parrot! While I was out in the yard, the parrot must have seen the light in the living room and come in through the open window.

5
10
15
20
25
30
35

A. Find the phrases or sentences in the reading which indicate the following:

1. The writer did not close the drapes.
2. The writer had some idea of where the cry for help was coming from.
3. The writer used the flashlight which he took with him into the yard.
4. The writer did not find anyone in the yard.
5. The parrot cried "Help!" soon after the writer came back into the room.

B. Answer the following questions in your own words. Use one complete sentence for each answer.

1. Why did the writer go into the yard?
2. What did the writer arm himself with before going out?
3. Why did the writer think that his imagination was playing tricks on him?
4. How many times did the writer hear the cry of "Help! Help!"?

C. Complete the following sentences. Your answers must be related to the ideas contained in the reading.

1. The writer turned on the light because _____ .
2. The writer thought, "Maybe one of the neighborhood children _____ ."
3. The writer found his son's baseball bat which

   _____ .
4. No sooner _____ than he was startled by the cry of "Help! Help!"
5. If the drapes had been closed, the parrot _____ .

D. Explain the meanings of the following words and phrases as they are used in the passage: engrossed (2); in trouble (15); come in handy (17); no sign (24); came to the conclusion (25); startled (31).

E. Composition   Imagine that you are a friend of the writer of this story. Write one paragraph which would form part of a longer letter written to a friend, and which tells of the parrot episode. Begin your paragraph: "By the way, I have to tell you about a very funny thing that happened to a friend of mine the other day." Do not introduce any ideas which are not in the reading. Use your own words as much as possible. Limit your paragraph to 120 words.

F. *Look at these sentences:*

It was *too dark for me to read* easily.
He ran *too fast for Marie to catch* him.
This pattern is *too* + adjective or adverb + *for* + (pro)noun + *to* + main form of the verb.

Now combine the following pairs of sentences to make one sentence. Follow this model:

The window was very small. He could not get through it.

The window was too small for him to get through.
(Notice that *it* is omitted.)

1. The suitcase was very heavy. She couldn't carry it.
2. These shoes are very small. I can't wear them.
3. The ocean was very rough. We couldn't go swimming.
4. The ice looks very thin. You can't walk on it.
5. He was speaking very quickly. We couldn't catch what he said.
6. The mailman came very late. We didn't get our letters before going on vacation.
7. It's very early. The children can't go to bed yet.
8. This soup is very hot. I can't drink it.
9. The man was very far away. We couldn't see his face clearly.
10. The window was very dirty. Nobody could see through it.

201 W. 87th Street
New York, N.Y. 10024
February 20, 1978

Dear Mr. Anderson:

I am not sure that you will remember me, but we met in 5
Bethany last year. It was at your daughter's wedding. Her
husband David is an old friend of mine (in fact, we were
roommates in college), and I came from New York for the
wedding. You and I had a long chat at the reception and I
told you a little about my job as a reporter for the *New York* 10
Times. You said that I should get in touch with you if I ever
decided to come back to Bethany.

At that time I had every intention of staying in New York,
but since then I have changed my mind and now I would like
very much to get a job back in my own hometown. My 15
problem is this—I have been away now for so long (since
1967, in fact) that I have no job contacts in Bethany. That is
why I am writing to you now. I would appreciate it very
much if you could put me in touch with anyone who could
help me or advise me. I hesitated writing to you like this, 20
but any suggestions you might have would be appreciated.
My best wishes to you and Mrs. Anderson.

Sincerely,
Patrick Neal

3271 Valley Road 25
Bethany, West Virginia 26032
February 24, 1978

Dear Patrick,

Of course I haven't forgotten you! I remembered who you
were as soon as I saw the return address on the envelope. By 30
some strange coincidence, my wife and I were talking about
you just the other day. You see, last week I had lunch with a
friend of mine who is the editor of the *Bethany Daily*
Express. He was worried because he is about to lose one of
his top reporters and so far he has not been able to find 35
anyone to replace him. He wants someone with broad
experience and preferably someone who was born and

brought up here. I immediately thought of you. I didn't
mention your name at the time, however, because last year
you seemed so determined to stay in New York. My wife   40
thought that I should write to you, just in case you might be
interested, but then I discovered that I had misplaced your
address. When your letter came yesterday, I called my friend
and told him about you. He said he would get a letter off to
you right away. You may have already heard from him.   45

This is really good news. I am glad you have decided to
move back to Bethany. I look forward to seeing you again.
My wife and I both send our best wishes.

Sincerely,
Bill Anderson   50

A. *Find the phrases or sentences in the letters which*
   indicate the following:
   1. Patrick Neal was not sure that Mr. Anderson would
      remember him.
   2. Patrick was brought up in Bethany.
   3. Patrick did not know many people in Bethany who
      could help him.
   4. There was a job opportunity for Patrick at the
      Bethany Daily Express.
   5. Mr. Anderson spoke to his friend about Patrick as
      soon as he got the letter.

B. *Answer the following questions in your own words. Use*
   one complete sentence for each answer.
   1. Why had Patrick Neal been invited to Mr. Anderson's
      daughter's wedding?
   2. How long had Patrick been working in New York?
   3. What did Patrick ask Mr. Anderson to do for him?
   4. What kind of journalist was the editor of the *Bethany*
      Daily Express looking for?

C. *Complete the following sentences. Your answers must*
   be related to the ideas contained in the reading.
   1. "Get in touch with me," Mr. Anderson had told
      Patrick Neal, "if _____."
   2. Patrick asked Mr. Anderson to _____ who could
      advise him.

3. Mr. Anderson thought Patrick wanted to stay in New York, so _____.
4. As soon as Patrick's letter arrived, _____.
5. "_____," the editor said, after Mr. Anderson told him about Neal.

D. *Explain the meanings of the following words and phrases as they are used in the reading:* *get in touch with* (11); *job contacts* (17); *appreciated* (21); *coincidence* (31); *brought up* (38); *determined* (40).

E. *Composition* Imagine that you are the editor of the *Bethany Daily Express*. Write a brief letter to Patrick Neal, saying that you had heard about him from Mr. Anderson and that you would like to invite him to come to Bethany for an interview. Limit your letter to 100 words.

F. *Look at this sentence:*

I have been away now for *so long that I have no contacts*.

In this pattern, notice *so* + adjective or adverb + result clause. The result clause is introduced by *that*, although it is usually omitted in spoken English. We use *such* instead of *so* when the result clause is preceded by a noun or noun phrase.

I have been away now for *such a long time that I have no contacts*.

Now combine each pair of sentences to form a result clause, following these models:

It was a rainy day. He could not go out.
It was such a rainy day (that) he could not go out.
I was tired. I could not walk any further.
I was so tired (that) I could not walk any further.

1. The book was dull. Tom couldn't finish it.
2. It's a difficult test. Almost nobody can pass it.
3. This is good soup. I think I'll have some more.
4. He looked sick. It was hard to recognize him.
5. It was a foggy night. We decided to stay indoors.
6. These flowers are inexpensive. I think I'll buy some more.

7. The road is bad. Almost nobody uses it anymore.
8. He's torn a big hole in his pants. He won't be able to patch them.
9. Everybody was quiet. I thought they had all gone to sleep.
10. Mary got up late. She almost missed her train.

After a quick breakfast in the coffee shop next to the hotel, John crossed the street and walked directly to the Becker Real Estate office. As he approached the glass-front office, he saw his reflection and paused to straighten his shirt collar and adjust his tie, pretending to be looking at the 5
large display of photographs visible through the glass. They were photographs of houses for sale and alongside each one was a small placard with a brief description of the property and the price. It was an excellent location for the office, he thought, and the display could not help but attract the 10
attention of people passing by there every day. Pausing at the door, he glanced at his watch. His appointment with Mr. Becker was at nine-fifteen, which was still another ten minutes, but he did not want to run the risk of being late the first day. The story his instructor, Miss Gatlin, had told of 15
the real estate salesman who lost an important sale because he was five minutes late for an appointment with a prospective client, had made an indelible impression on him. Punctuality, Miss Gatlin had emphasized over and over again, was essential in business. 20

John opened the door and surveyed the office in one quick glance. It was a large, tastefully decorated room with comfortable-looking furniture arranged more like a living room than an office, which was all-important, he realized, in creating the kind of friendly and relaxed atmosphere that 25
makes clients instantly feel at home. Over on one side was the receptionist's desk and beyond that, covering the whole back area, were rows of desks for the sales staff. As he walked up to the receptionist's desk, he could not help but wonder which of the desks he would be assigned to. "You're 30
early for your appointment," the receptionist said after he identified himself. "Mr. Becker hasn't arrived yet, but you can have a seat over there and wait for him," she told him, pointing to the first desk in the third row. "Mr. Becker said that one will be yours." 35

John settled into the comfortable swivel chair behind the desk and leaned the chair back gently, hardly able to believe his good fortune. In a few minutes he began to get acquainted with his new desk, opening each of the drawers in turn and mentally trying to decide what he was going to 40 put in each of them. Suddenly he became aware of the fact that someone had entered the office and was talking to the receptionist.

"I'm terribly sorry, Mr. Yates," the receptionist was saying, "but Mr. Becker hasn't come in yet." 45

John had been so engrossed that he had lost track of the time and was amazed to see by his watch that it was already nine-fifty.

"My appointment with Mr. Becker was at nine forty-five," the elderly man said, obviously greatly annoyed, then 50 turned to leave. "I'm not going to wait any longer."

The receptionist was standing now. "Would you like to leave a message for Mr. Becker?" she asked. "Yes," he said as he opened the door. "Tell Mr. Becker I've changed my mind about buying that building on Sinclair Street." 55

"Mr. Yates!" John blurted out as he jumped to his feet. "Perhaps I can help you. My name is John Blake." Mr. Yates hesitated for a moment, then pushed the door closed again and came back toward John who was now standing by the receptionist's desk. "Mr. Blake, did you say?" said the 60 elderly man as he shook hands with John. "Yes, perhaps you can help me. You seem to be the only member of the staff on time today. I admire punctuality." John smiled and turned to the receptionist. "Get me the file on the Sinclair Street property, please," he said as he motioned Mr. Yates toward 65 his desk.

A. Find the phrases or sentences in the reading which indicate the following:

1. John had not spent much time over breakfast.
2. John was not actually looking at the photographs in the window.
3. John would always remember Miss Gatlin's story.
4. John wasn't sure which desk would be his.
5. Mr. Yates was clearly upset.

B. Answer the following questions in your own words. Use one complete sentence for each answer.

1. At what time did John pause at the door to look at his watch?
2. How long did John survey the office after opening the door?

3. Why did a real estate agent lose a big sale, according to Miss Gatlin?
4. What was it about John that Mr. Yates admired?

C. *Complete the following sentences. Your answers must be related to the ideas contained in the reading.*
   1. John seemed to be looking at the photographs in the window, but actually _____.
   2. People would be attracted to the office in the photograph because _____.
   3. John was told to take a seat at his new desk because he _____ and Mr. Becker _____.
   4. "Give _____ desk _____ John Blake tomorrow," said Mr. Becker.
   5. "_____, Mr. Yates," said John as the receptionist went to get the file on the Sinclair Street property.

D. *Explain the meanings of the following words and phrases as they are used in the reading:* visible (6); placard (8); run the risk of (14); a prospective client (18); swivel (36); blurted out (56).

E. **Composition**   Imagine that you are the receptionist. Write a short letter to a friend describing what happened from the time John Blake entered the office until he took Mr. Yates over to his new desk. Use your own words as much as possible. Limit your letter to 120 words.

F. *Look at this sentence:*
      The display *could not help but* attract attention.
   This means that the display was bound to attract attention because it was so attractive. Here is another example:
      The neighbors *can't help but* hear every word you're saying.
   This means the neighbors are bound to hear every word because you're talking so loud.

   Now rewrite these sentences using can/could not help but.
   1. The boy's mother noticed the broken window.

2. Young children ask a lot of questions.
3. The waiter knows that we're ready to order now.
4. The lazy real estate salesman lost the client.
5. They'll see him now because he's standing up.
6. She overheard what they were saying at the next table.
7. The small child bruised himself climbing the tree.
8. Married couples argue from time to time.
9. We're going to get wet in this downpour.
10. He was so good that they gave him first prize.

Joe was looking forward to his first trip by *Thunderbolt*, as the space shuttle to the moon was called. He had heard a great deal about the trip from his friends who had already been on the shuttle. They all advised him to go during the winter, not during the summer. But Joe is the kind of 5 person who listens to everybody's advice and then does exactly what he had planned to do in the first place.

Joe entered the space station shortly after three o'clock on a Friday afternoon in the middle of July. This was a particularly bad time to take a flight because all during the 10 month of July, guided tours of schoolchildren from all over the United States flood into Cape Ortega to take advantage of the special summer discount rates for students. He had to join one of the long lines of young students who were waiting their turn for the preflight examination. When Joe's turn 15 came to step up to the computerized panel, he had a difficult time figuring out how the controls on the analyzer worked and how to get the door on the analyzer chamber to open so that he could step in. The people in the long line behind him began to grumble impatiently at the delay, but he finally 20 completed the examination sequence and received the printout of the results on a blue data card. The card verified that he was approved for space travel.

Shortly before six o'clock, Joe completed all of the preflight routines, including the required security clearance of his baggage. By asking directions from several young students, he managed to find the briefing rooms. As he entered the briefing area, he saw that there were lighted signs over the doors to two briefing rooms, and he noticed that both signs were blinking on and off, indicating that the sessions were about to begin. One of the signs said, "6:00 P.M. Briefing" and the other said, "6:05 P.M. Briefing." He was trying to decide which room to enter when, all of a sudden, he was caught up in a crowd of enthusiastic young students who were pushing and shoving their way into the rooms. He was swept along until at one point as he neared the door, he was pushed sideways into the lines of people entering Room C. Just as they moved through the doorway into the room, the automatic doors began to close. Once inside, he was relieved to see that there were no schoolchildren there. After spending the last two or three hours in preflight routines with hundreds of children, he was beginning to understand why all his friends had advised him not to travel in the summer, and he was delighted to join a briefing session with people more his own age. Some of them, as a matter of fact, were considerably older than he was.

The briefing session, which consisted of talks, demonstrations and short films, lasted two hours. At the conclusion of the session, they were transported directly to the launch area where crewmembers were waiting to put them aboard the spaceship.

Since this was his first space flight, Joe was nervous at first. But once the launch had been successfully completed and the ship had achieved the initial orbit around Earth, he relaxed and sat back to enjoy the flight. A few minutes later the Captain's voice came over the speaker system. "Our present speed," he began, "is twenty-four thousand two hundred and fifty miles per hour, giving us an Earth orbit time of forty-seven minutes." Joe smiled. He had some idea now how the pioneer astronauts must have felt a hundred years ago when they orbited the earth for the first time. The Captain continued, "Our flight time will be nine months, two weeks, six days and seventeen hours. We will be . . ." Suddenly Joe sat upright in his seat. Something was radically wrong. His total flight time, including transit time on the moon, was only supposed to be seven days. He immediately pressed the call button. When a flight attendant appeared at his side, he said, "This is the shuttle to the moon, isn't it?" The attendant looked at him in surprise and replied, "The Moon shuttle? Oh no, sir. This flight is going to Mars!"

A. **Find the phrases or sentences in the reading which indicate the following:**
   1. Joe had great expectations about his first space flight.
   2. Schoolchildren crowded into Cape Ortega to make use of summer discount rates for students.
   3. Other passengers were quietly complaining about Joe.
   4. Joe no longer felt burdened by the crowds of children.
   5. Joe guessed how the first astronauts probably felt a century before.

B. **Answer the following questions in your own words. Use one complete sentence for each answer.**
   1. Why was the month of July a bad month to go to the moon?
   2. Why were the people behind Joe grumbling?
   3. What age group would you say Joe's fellow travelers to Mars belonged to?
   4. When did Joe begin to relax on his flight?

C. **Complete the following sentences. Your answers must be related to the ideas contained in the reading.**
   1. All of Joe's friends advised him to travel in the winter, but _____.
   2. "_____," said some of the students who were standing behind Joe.
   3. The following words were printed on the blue data card: "_____."
   4. Joe did not know that Room C _____.
   5. Joe pushed the call button because _____.

D. **Explain the meanings of the following words and phrases as they are used in the reading:** *figuring out* (17); *verified* (22); *security clearance* (25); *enthusiastic* (34); *a briefing session* (45); *radically* (66).

E. Composition You are Joe. Write a brief letter to one of your friends on Earth. This letter, which will be sent by radio from your Mars flight, should contain a description of what happened to you from the time you completed all of your preflight routines until the flight attendant informed you of your destination. Use your own words as much as possible. Limit your composition to 100 words.

F. Look at these sentences:

He had a difficult time figuring out *how to get the door open*.

He didn't know *where to put it*.

The *to* + verb (main form) pattern often follows question words such as *how, where, what, when, whose*.

Now complete each sentence below by using an appropriate verb from the list.

buy	open	fly
get down	pick	wait
get	pronounce	wear
look for		

1. Let's ask the policeman over there how _____ to the post office.
2. She's still trying to decide which dress _____ to the party.
3. He lost his pen and doesn't know where _____ it.
4. Have you been told which flowers _____?
5. Keep your eyes closed. I'll tell you when _____ them.
6. The boy has climbed up on the roof and doesn't know how _____.
7. I've been trying to find out where _____ a new calculator.
8. Would you mind telling me how _____ this word?
9. She already left. No one told her how long _____.
10. The Browns still haven't decided which airline _____.

When I got to the airport, I discovered that the plane from Chicago, which my brother was traveling on, had been delayed in Denver because of engine trouble and was expected to be about an hour late. Usually when I have to wait around the airport to meet a flight, I go to the observation deck and pass the time by watching planes land and take off, but that particular evening I had a splitting headache, which I thought the noise of jet engines might make worse. Therefore, I decided to walk around inside the terminal for a while.

As I was walking by the shops on the lower level, I happened to see a display of flight bags, which somehow reminded me all of a sudden of my briefcase and I realized that I was not carrying it now. Quickly I thought back, trying to remember where I might have left it. Realizing that I had not stopped anyplace since I left the airline ticket counter, I concluded I must have put it down there so I immediately hurried back to the main terminal to get it. When I finally reached the counter, I looked all around but my briefcase was nowhere in sight. At first I was sure that somebody had just walked off with it, but then I realized there was a chance that whoever found it might have turned it in at the counter. I patiently waited in line for my turn at

the counter and then I described the briefcase and asked if
by any chance it had been turned in. The agent shook his   25
head. At that moment I happened to glance over his shoulder
at the conveyor belt that was moving baggage from the
check-in counter down to the loading platforms and I
shrieked, "There it is!" But just as the agent turned to look,
the briefcase reached the end of the conveyor belt and   30
vanished from view down the chute.

"Did you see your briefcase?" the agent wanted to know.

"Yes!" I exclaimed. "It just went through that opening
over there. How do I get it back now?"

"That's no problem," replied the agent. "Just give me your   35
baggage claim check and I think we can catch it before it's
loaded on a flight."

"But I don't have a claim check!" I sputtered. "I didn't
check it! I'm not going anywhere! I'm just here to meet a
flight." Calming myself down a bit, I explained what I had   40
done and suggested that it had undoubtedly been turned in
at the counter and that one of the agents had probably
checked it with other baggage and placed it on the conveyor
belt.

The agent told me that the only way he could trace it   45
would be to have a claim form with a description of what the
briefcase looked like. By the time I filled out the form and
the agent called down to the baggage area, my briefcase
along with all the other baggage had already been loaded on
one of the flights, but they could not be sure which one. The   50
agent took my phone number and assured me they would
call as soon as they located the briefcase, and that even
though I lived in Sioux City, which was an hour-and-a-half
drive away, they would deliver it to my address as soon as
they got it back.   55

In the meantime, my brother's flight had arrived and,
after getting his suitcases, we headed for my car in the
parking lot. During the drive home I had plenty of time to
tell him all about my unfortunate experience. When we got
home and were unloading the car, I could hardly believe my   60
eyes when my brother brought a briefcase out of the car,
which he had found on the floor in the back seat. It was the
briefcase I thought I had lost, but which obviously I had
never taken into the airport in the first place! I realized that
at that moment the airline people were painstakingly   65

checking each piece of luggage on their Denver, St. Louis and Chicago flights, looking for my briefcase, and I dreaded the thought of having to call them and tell them I had found it in my car.

The telephone was ringing as we walked in the house. 70 Answering it, I was shocked when an airline employee identified himself and said, "We have good news for you! We located your briefcase in Denver and it is already aboard another flight coming back. It should be in at eleven o'clock and will be delivered to you shortly after midnight by 75 special messenger."

A. *Find the phrases or sentences in the reading which indicate the following:*
   1. The display of flight bags made the writer remember that he no longer had his briefcase.
   2. The writer concluded that he had not stopped in the air terminal except at the ticket counter.
   3. The writer couldn't see his briefcase anywhere.
   4. The writer told the agent he was sure someone had checked his briefcase in with other luggage.
   5. The prospect of telling the airline that he had found his briefcase in the car made him fearful and anxious.

B. *Answer the following questions in your own words. Use one complete sentence for each answer.*
   1. Why did the writer go to the airport?
   2. Why didn't the writer want to watch the planes landing and taking off?
   3. How did the agent respond when the writer asked if his briefcase had been turned in?
   4. Why couldn't the airline find the briefcase at the airport?

C. *Complete the following sentences. Your answers must be related to the ideas contained in the reading.*
   1. When the writer saw the flight bags, he _____ .
   2. When his turn finally came at the counter, the writer asked the agent, "_____?"
   3. Only after the briefcase entered the chute did the agent _____ .
   4. After the agent said he would call when they found the briefcase, he said, "_____ ."

D. Explain the meanings of the following words and phrases as they are used in the reading: *splitting* (7); *my turn* (23); *shrieked* (29); *chute* (31); *sputtered* (38); *in the first place* (64).

E. Composition   You are the ticket agent. Write a report to your superior describing what took place between you and the writer. Begin at the time the writer first told you about the briefcase, and end with a phone call from the airline employee who told the writer about the "second" briefcase. You may want to add a surprise ending of your own. Limit the report to 130 words.

F. Compare these two sentences:

I had a splitting headache, *which I thought the noise of jet engines might make worse.*

I happened to glance at the conveyor belt *that was moving the baggage to the loading platforms.*

In the first, the relative clause, which is set off by a comma, provides additional information which is non-essential to the meaning; in the second, the relative clause is *not* set off by a comma because it provides important or essential information.

Now combine each pair of sentences below to make one sentence. Follow the models:

Mr. Smith died last week. He used to live next door to us.

Mr. Smith, who used to live next door to us, died last week.

I bought some red wine. It tasted sour.

The red wine _____ .

The red wine (that) I bought tasted sour.

1. The *Lark* was late. It should have arrived at 3:15.
2. He made a promise. He didn't keep it. _____ the promise _____ .
3. My son starts school in September. He'll be five years old next month.
4. I waved to a man just now. He's my supervisor. The man _____ .
5. This author is very popular now. No one had heard of him twenty years ago.

6. We saw a famous actor on TV last night. What's his name? _____ of the famous actor _____?
7. The lawyer's evidence proved to be false. It looked very convincing when first presented.
8. My brother tells jokes. We don't like them. _____ the jokes _____.
9. The big truck crashed into a house. It happened to be fully loaded.
10. Susan met a man at a dance. She fell in love with him. _____ a man _____.

A LIBRARY MISHAP

The silence of the Reference Room in the university library was broken only by an occasional cough and now and then by the scarcely audible sound of pages being turned. There were about twenty people in the room, most of them with their heads bent over their books. The assistant librarian who was in charge of the room sat at a desk in one corner. She glanced at Phil as he came in, then went on with her work.

Phil had never been to this part of the library before, and he wondered why it had not been included in the tour for freshman students last week. He reached in his pocket and pulled out a scrap of paper on which he had scribbled the title and call number of the book he was supposed to read. Then he walked around the room almost on tiptoe, afraid of disturbing the serious readers with his heavy shoes. The shelves were filled with thick volumes: dictionaries in many languages, encyclopedias, atlases, biographies and other works. Off in one corner he finally found the section he was looking for. The books in this section were on a high shelf out of his reach, but he located a small stepladder over by the encyclopedias and quietly moved it into position. Unfortunately, as he was coming back down the ladder, the book he had taken off the shelf slipped out of his hand and fell to the floor with a loud crash. Everybody in the library looked up at him at the same time, obviously annoyed by the disturbance. Phil felt his face turn red as he picked up his book, which luckily did not seem to have been damaged by the fall.

He had just sat down at one of the tables when he found the young library assistant standing next to him. "You must be more careful handling these books," she whispered softly. Satisfied that she had done her duty, she turned to go back to her desk. Phil opened his book and started to leaf through it. Then he stopped and looked closely at one of the pages. It was in Latin! Somehow he had managed to get the wrong book. "Oh no!" he blurted out without thinking. His voice shattered the silence of the room and all of a sudden everyone was glaring at him. He winced as he realized what he had done. Glancing quickly around the room, he tried to

make a silent apology, forming the words "I'm sorry" with   40
his lips.

Since the call number he had written down was obviously
incorrect, Phil concluded that he would have to look up the
correct number in the card catalog. Leaving the book on the
table, he tiptoed over to the card catalog file and looked   45
down row after row of drawers arranged in alphabetical
order until he found the right one. Then he pulled the
drawer out carefully and started thumbing through the
cards, looking for the title of his book. The card he was
looking for was the next-to-last one at the back of the   50
drawer. As he turned to reach for a piece of note paper to jot
down the number, his thumb caught the front edge of the
drawer, pulling it out of its compartment. Phil grabbed for
the drawer, but it was too late.

A. *Say whether the following statements are true or false*
   and give the phrases or sentences from the passage
   which indicate this.
   1. There was a lot of noise in the Reference Room.
   2. The assistant librarian did not take much notice of
      Phil when he came in.
   3. Phil was well acquainted with the Reference Room.
   4. Phil wanted a book written in Latin.
   5. The card catalog drawer fell with a loud crash.

B. *Answer the following questions in your own words. Use*
   one complete sentence for each answer.
   1. How did Phil walk so as not to disturb the other
      readers?
   2. Where was the section of books that Phil was looking
      for?
   3. What made Phil's face turn red?
   4. Why was the drawer in such a position that the slight
      movement of Phil's thumb would cause it to fall?

C. *Complete the following sentences. Your answers must*
   be related to the ideas contained in the reading.
   1. Most of the books on the shelves, such as, _____,
      were not the objects of Phil's search.
   2. Phil would not have disturbed the readers if _____.
   3. Although the book fell hard, it _____.

4. The library assistant cautioned Phil to _____ .
5. Phil had to use the card catalog because _____ .

D. *Explain the meanings of the following words and phrases as they are used in the reading:* on tiptoe (14); done her duty (32); leaf through (33); blurted out (36); winced (38); thumbing through (48).

E. *Composition*   Imagine that you are the assistant librarian. Describe what you did and said from the time Phil dropped the book until he caused the card catalog drawer to fall to the floor. Make up an ending which tells the reader what you would say to Phil following this third disturbance. Use your own words as much as possible. Limit your composition to 110 words.

F. *Look at this sentence:*
    Phil felt his face *turn red*.
Notice that the adjective *red* describing *face* follows the verb. Here are two more examples:
    As we climbed higher, it *got colder*.
    She *looks* remarkably *young*.

Now complete the following sentences by choosing a suitable verb and adjective from the list below. Be sure to put the verb into the correct form.

come true	go bad	look different
fall ill	grow taller	run out
feel tired	keep quiet	smell good
get dark		

1. It must be very late. It's already beginning to _____ .
2. John _____ seriously _____ and was taken to the hospital.
3. I'm surprised you don't _____ after working so hard.
4. The teacher asked us to _____ while he went out of the classroom.
5. I wonder what they're cooking. It certainly _____ .
6. Your daughter _____ much _____ since I last saw her.

7. He forgot to put the milk in the refrigerator, so it
_____ .

8. Simon had to come back early from his vacation
because he _____ of money.

9. I didn't recognize my daughter in her new Air Force
uniform. She _____ quite _____ .

10. He always wanted to be an actor—and now his wish
_____ .

After lunch, without waiting to get permission from their parents, the two young boys set off to explore Pirate's Cove, which somebody said was on the other side of the rocks at the south end of the beach. They persuaded their five-year-old sister to stay behind, telling her that climbing around the rocks would be too dangerous for her. It was low tide and they managed to pick their way around the jagged rocks without too much difficulty. Once they got on the other side, the beach along Pirate's Cove stretched endlessly in front of them. It was like discovering a new world. They imagined that they were pirates, and they found exciting things to do. There were damp, dark caves to explore, and they half expected to come across smugglers hiding in each one; there were innumerable pools among the rocks, full of small fish and strange creatures; and scattered along the beach were oil drums and other objects washed up and left by the tide, which they pretended were pirate treasures.

The afternoon passed quickly and the sun was already beginning to go down when the two boys reluctantly decided to head back. But long before they reached the rocks, they could see that the tide had come in so far that they were now cut off from the other part of the beach. They looked at each other in dismay. It was useless to go on since there was

clearly no way of getting around the rocks that divided the
beach. If, on the other hand, they went back the way they   25
had just come, the tide would be in long before they could
reach the end of the long stretch of beach. Their only chance
of escape was to find a way up the cliff, which did not seem to
be too steep in some places. At least they might be able to
climb high enough to be out of reach of the pounding waves   30
which were getting closer all the time.

In less than ten minutes, they found a path which seemed
to lead all the way up to the top of the cliff. But by no means
were their troubles over. Halfway up, the path was blocked
by a large rock which seemed impossible to get over. The two   35
boys glanced back down the steep cliff and realized they
would never be able to get down without slipping and
falling. They had no choice now. Hoping that someone
walking along the edge of the cliff might hear them, they
started shouting at the top of their lungs. They were both   40
surprised when their father's face appeared over the edge of
the cliff. He called to them and told them not to move until
he came back. A few minutes later he reappeared with two
other men. They lowered ropes over the edge and the two
boys, holding on tightly to the ropes, were pulled up to   45
safety. At the top of the cliff, they found their worried
mother and father and their little sister. She had told their
parents where the boys had gone and had saved them from
spending a terrifying night on the cliff.

*A. Say whether the following statements are true or false
and indicate which phrases or sentences indicate this.*
   1. The boys knew Pirate's Cove well.
   2. The boys did not want to go home.
   3. Having considered the alternatives, the boys decided
      that they had to climb the cliff.
   4. The boys did not shout very loud.
   5. The boys' father climbed down to rescue them.

*B. Answer the following questions in your own words. Use
one complete sentence for each answer.*
   1. How did the boys spend their time in Pirate's Cove?
   2. Why did the two boys look at each other in dismay?
   3. Why couldn't the two boys get to the top of the cliff?

4. How did their parents know where to look for the two boys?

C. Complete the following sentences. Your answers must be related to the ideas contained in the reading.
1. "_____," the two boys said to their little sister. "_____."
2. While the two boys were exploring Pirate's Cove, the tide _____.
3. "If we go back the same way we came," the boys thought, "the tide _____."
4. If the path had not been blocked by a rock, the two boys _____.
5. "_____," the boys' father told them.

D. Explain the meanings of the following words and phrases as they are used in the reading: *persuaded* (4); *low tide* (6); *reluctantly* (19); *steep* (29); *by no means* (33); *at the top of their lungs* (40).

E. Composition   Imagine that you are one of the boys trapped on the beach. Describe what you did from the time you were cut off by the tide until you finally reached the top of the cliff. Do not include any ideas which are not in the reading. Use your own words as much as possible. Limit your composition to 100 words.

F. Look at this sentence:
    They *persuaded their five-year-old sister to stay behind.*
The sentence pattern here is verb + (pro)noun + *to* + verb (main form). Here are two more examples:
    The landlord *asked me to pay* a week's rent in advance.
    The teacher *told the class not to make* so much noise.

Now complete the following sentences with an appropriate noun or pronoun, and the correct form of a verb from the list below.

buy	lose	read
work	marry	spend
eat	put	use
lock		

1. We never expected _____ his temper.
2. My parents asked _____ not _____ the girl I love.
3. Will you remind _____ the door before I go to bed?
4. The Smiths have invited _____ a weekend with them.
5. I hope you told _____ our suitcases in Room 113.
6. Of course you feel sick! We warned _____ not _____ so much ice cream.
7. I want _____ these instructions carefully.
8. Why did you advise _____ that old car?
9. Mrs. Roberts has been trying to persuade _____ in her garden.
10. The teacher didn't allow _____ a dictionary during the test.

Mr. Foster motioned towards the chair on the other side of the desk and told Henry to take a seat. "I'm waiting for a call from Atlanta," he explained. The telephone rang just as he spoke. He picked up the receiver and spoke rapidly and impatiently into the telephone. Henry, meanwhile, was 5
tense and nervous. For days he had dreaded the thought of this interview and now he wanted to get it over with as soon as possible. Having to wait like this just prolonged the agony. When Mr. Foster finished, his secretary came in with a big stack of letters. "I really won't keep you waiting much 10
longer," said Mr. Foster apologetically, as he picked up the first letter and began to read it. "But these have to go out right away."

Henry tried to calm his nerves by examining Mr. Foster's office in detail. On his right there was a large window with a 15
view of the factory yard. Henry could see two men on a forklift moving across the yard toward what seemed to be a large warehouse. Close to the window there were three chairs arranged around one end of a long conference table, with a pitcher of water and some glasses on the table. To 20
Henry's left there were bookshelves covering the whole wall from floor to ceiling. The shelves were empty except for a dozen or so books, a pile of technical journals, which looked

as if they might topple off the shelf at any moment, and a
plastic duck standing by itself on the top shelf and looking a   25
bit out of place in an executive's office. Henry could not help
wondering how it got there.

The most impressive piece of furniture in the room was
Mr. Foster's desk. Everything on its polished top was
arranged neatly. On either side of the desk there were two   30
metal trays, one marked IN, and the other marked OUT,
into which Mr. Foster was tossing letters as he signed them.

Henry finished his survey of the room just as Mr. Foster
signed the last letter. "That's all of them," he said, as he
buzzed for his secretary to come in and get them. Then he   35
took off his glasses and rubbed his eyes. "Now let me see," he
said. "You've come about our ad for a clerk in the accounting
department, haven't you?" Henry nodded. His interview had
begun.

A. *Say whether the following statements are true or false*
   and indicate which phrases or sentences from the
   passage indicate this.
   1. Henry would have preferred his interview to begin
      immediately.
   2. The secretary waited in the room while Mr. Foster
      signed the letters.
   3. The technical journals were very carefully arranged
      on the top shelf.
   4. Mr. Foster's desk was arranged very neatly.
   5. Mr. Foster had no idea what job Henry had come for.

B. *Answer the following questions in your own words. Use*
   one complete sentence for each answer.
   1. How did Mr. Foster show Henry where to sit?
   2. Why did Mr. Foster want to sign the letters before he
      interviewed Henry?
   3. What was happening in the factory yard when Henry
      looked out the window?
   4. What did Henry think was "out of place" in the office?

C. *Complete the following sentences. Your answers must*
   be related to the ideas contained in the reading.
   1. The phone rang just as Mr. Foster was explaining
      that _____ .

2. The bookshelves were so large that _____ .
3. "_____ ," thought Henry as he looked at the toy duck.
4. After signing each letter, he tossed it _____ .
5. Henry nodded when Mr. Foster asked him whether

_____ .

D. Explain the meanings of the following words and phrases as they are used in the reading: *get it over with* (7); *prolonged the agony* (8); *apologetically* (11); *topple off* (24); *out of place* (26); *buzzed for* (35).

E. Composition   Imagine that you are Henry. Describe what you did from the time you came into the room until your interview began. Do not include any ideas which are not in the passage. Use your own words as much as possible. Limit your composition to 100 words.

F. Look at this sentence:

Henry could *see* two men on a forklift *moving* across the yard.

In this pattern, the verb of perception (*see, hear, notice,* etc.) is followed by an object (noun or pronoun) + verb-*ing*. The use of the -*ing* form of a verb in this pattern indicates that the action is continuous. Compare this to the pattern in which the use of the main form of the verb (see Exercise G on page 30) indicates that the action is completed.

Henry *saw* the men on the forklift *move* across the yard.

The (pro)noun + verb-*ing* pattern is also used with verbs such as *find, keep* and *catch,* as in line 10:

I really won't *keep* you *waiting* much longer.

Now complete the following sentences by choosing an appropriate verb from the list below.

burn	lie	steal
chase	bake	swim
come	play	wait
have	sign	

1. I can hear someone _____ up the stairs.
2. We saw the girls _____ in the lake.
3. I think I smell something _____ in the kitchen.
4. He noticed a letter _____ on the floor just as he was opening the door.
5. The children watched their father _____ the cake.
6. Just look at the cat _____ the birds.
7. The manager kept Henry _____ until he had finished _____ all the letters.
8. Can you imagine yourself _____ the part of Hamlet?
9. The librarian caught a boy _____ books from the library.
10. I found them already _____ dinner when I got there.

The party started shortly after nine. Mr. Wood, who lived
in the apartment below, sighed to himself as he heard the
first signs — the steady tramp of feet on the stairs and the
sound of excited voices as the guests greeted each other. He
knew that in just a few minutes the music would begin and, 5
after that, the dancing. Luckily, Mr. Wood had brought some
work home from the office which would keep him busy for a
while, perhaps for a couple of hours or so. He hoped this
would help him ignore the party that was going on upstairs.

By eleven o'clock Mr. Wood felt very tired. He was ready 10
for bed but he knew from past experience that he was not
going to be able to get to sleep. Putting on his pajamas, he
propped himself up in bed with a book. He tried to
concentrate on his book, but the noise from the room directly
above his head was too much. He found himself reading the 15
same page over and over again. Giving up, he turned out the
light and buried his head in the pillows in a desperate effort
to shut out the noise. Finally, after what seemed like hours,
he switched the light back on and looked at his watch. It was
a little after three o'clock. He was furious. Throwing back 20
the covers, he jumped out of bed, put on his robe and
marched out of the bedroom and across the living room to
the front door of his apartment. He jerked the door open and
charged out into the hallway, heading for the stairs.

Gasping for breath after running up the stairs, Mr. Wood 25
positioned himself at his neighbor's door and knocked
several times as loud as he could. But no one opened the door.
This did not improve his temper. So he pounded on the door
and shouted, "Open up in there!" A moment later the door
opened and his neighbor, dressed in pajamas and rubbing 30
his eyes, appeared in the doorway. Recognizing Mr. Wood
and sensing that something terrible had happened, he asked,
"What is it, Mr. Wood? What's the matter? Is the place on
fire or something?" "No!" shouted Mr. Wood. "It's all this
noise! How do you expect people to get any sleep?" His 35
neighbor looked surprised and said, "What noise?" Mr. Wood
stopped and listened for a moment. There was silence. He
turned around slowly and looked up and down the empty
hallway, and then turned back and leaned his head through
the open doorway. "Where are all your guests?" he asked 40

with a puzzled look on his face. "They've gone home," said
his neighbor, opening the door wide and motioning with his
arm to the dark living room. "We had a little party earlier,
but everybody left a couple of hours ago," he explained. "I've
been in bed asleep." Mr. Wood could hardly believe it. There   45
was not another soul in the place. Then it suddenly dawned
on him that he must have gone off to sleep without realizing
it hours ago while the party was still going on. Feeling a
little foolish and quite embarrassed, Mr. Wood apologized for
waking up his neighbor in the middle of the night and   50
silently made his way back to his own apartment.

A. *Say whether the following statements are true or false
and indicate which phrases or sentences from the
passage indicate this.*
1. Mr. Wood hoped the work he brought home from the
   office would help him ignore the party.
2. This was not the first time that there had been a
   party of this kind in the apartment upstairs.
3. Mr. Wood did not even try to get to sleep.
4. Mr. Wood was angry when he went upstairs to
   complain.
5. The guests all promised to be quieter after Mr. Wood's
   visit.

B. *Answer the following questions in your own words. Use
one complete sentence for each answer.*
1. How did Mr. Wood manage to ignore the noise of the
   party until he went to bed?
2. How long did Mr. Wood think that the party had been
   going on when he went upstairs to complain?
3. How was the party host dressed when Mr. Wood
   confronted him?
4. Why did Mr. Wood's anger suddenly vanish?

C. *Complete the following sentences. Your answers must
be related to the ideas contained in the reading.*
1. The noise from the room directly over Mr. Wood's
   head prevented him _____ .
2. Although Mr. Wood buried his head in the pillows,
   _____ .

3. Although Mr. Wood knocked on the door several times, _____ .
4. The host guessed that something terrible had happened, so he asked Mr. Wood whether _____ .
5. "_____," said Mr. Wood before silently making his way back to his own apartment.

D. *Explain the meanings of the following words and phrases as they are used in the reading:* sighed (2); tramp (3); propped himself up (13); giving up (16); desperate (17); soul (46).

E. *Composition* Imagine that you are Mr. Wood. Describe what you did from the time you jumped out of bed until you came back to your room after talking to your neighbor. Do not introduce any ideas that are not in the passage. Use your own words as much as possible. Limit your composition to 100 words.

F. *Look at this sentence:*
Putting on his pajamas, he propped himself up in bed.
In the reading there are several sentences which include a phrase beginning with verb-*ing*. You often have the choice of using a phrase beginning with verb-*ing* when the subject of the phrase is the same as the subject of the main sentence.
See further examples of these phrases in lines 16, 20, 25, 31-32, 42, 48.

Change the time clauses in the sentences below to phrases beginning with verb-ing.
1. When I was walking down the street the other day, I happened to notice a wallet lying on the sidewalk.
2. When Bill arrived at Mrs. Carter's house, he was surprised to find her gone.
3. When he realized that he needed to get help, he rushed out of the house.
4. While she was sitting at the counter, she suddenly remembered she had to buy cough medicine.
5. When I turned to go back to my seat, I happened to notice my ex-neighbor.

6. When I reached the hotel, I registered and went straight to my room.
7. As soon as I emptied the suitcases, I left the room.
8. After she searched through a number of drawers, Miss Lee found the key to the attic.
9. He picked up the monkey and, while he held it close to him, he began to cry.
10. As he leaned on the doctor's shoulder and walked slowly, he was led off to the ship's hospital.

A LONG, RAINY NIGHT

Mr. Price, the owner of an antique store in Daly City, lived
alone in a small apartment above his store. Because of the
many valuable articles he kept on the premises, he was
always afraid that one night somebody might break into his
store. Years before, when he had first opened his small shop   5
there, he had iron bars fitted to all the windows and double
locks put on all the doors. As an added safety measure, he
had special cabinets built so that he could lock up his most
valuable objects every night. But in spite of these
precautions, he never felt safe, especially when he had a lot   10
of money in the store after a good day's business.

One Friday night when he counted his money after closing
up, he found that he had taken in nearly a thousand dollars
that day. This was an exceptionally large sum of money and
the thought of keeping it in the store over the weekend made   15
him very nervous. He knew that it would be better to take it
over to his son's house where there was a small safe, but it
was raining hard that night and his son lived all the way on
the other side of town. Deciding not to venture out in the
rain, he took the money with him to his bedroom, put it in   20
the pocket of his overcoat and locked the coat in the closet.
He put the key to the closet under his pillow and went to
bed.

Mr. Price lay awake for a long time wondering if his
money was really safe, and it was well after midnight before   25
he fell asleep. Almost immediately, or so it seemed, he was
awakened by the loud ringing of the doorbell downstairs. He
sat up in bed. Could he have been dreaming? Surely, he
thought, no one could want to see him at this hour of the
night. The doorbell rang again, echoing through the   30
two-story building. He could not help thinking of a program
he had seen on television about a man who had been
attacked and robbed when he went to answer the door
during the night. Once again the doorbell rang, more
persistently this time.   35

Mr. Price got out of bed and went over to the window. The
rain had let up slightly. He opened the window and looked
out. He could just make out the shadowy figure of a man
standing on the sidewalk below. "What do you want?" Mr.
Price called out in a shaky voice. The man stepped back   40

until he was standing under the street light. It was a policeman. "Sorry to disturb you," said the policeman, "but all the lights are on in your store. At first I thought something was wrong, but everything seems to be all right. I guess you just forgot to turn them off when you closed up." 45

A. *Say whether the following statements are true or false and indicate which phrases or sentences from the passage indicate this.*
  1. It was not usual for Mr. Price to have a thousand dollars in the house after a good business day.
  2. Mr. Price locked up the money in his bedroom safe.
  3. It took Mr. Price a long time to get to sleep.
  4. Mr. Price did not think it was safe to answer the door at night.
  5. Mr. Price saw the police officer as soon as he looked out of the window.

B. *Answer the following questions in your own words. Use one complete sentence for each answer.*
  1. What precautions had Mr. Price taken to prevent anyone from breaking into his store?
  2. Why didn't Mr. Price take the money to his son's house?
  3. How many times did the doorbell ring?
  4. Why did the police officer disturb Mr. Price?

C. *Complete the following sentences. Your answers must be related to the ideas contained in the reading.*
  1. The special cabinets in which _____ had been specially made for this purpose.
  2. Instead of taking the money to his son's house, Mr. Price _____ .
  3. When Mr. Price first woke up, he wondered _____ .
  4. Mr. Price could not clearly see who was at the door until _____ .
  5. The policeman apologized for _____ .

114

D. Explain the meanings of the following words and phrases as they are used in the reading: *measure* (7); *precautions* (10); *venture out* (19); *echoing* (30); *persistently* (35); *let up* (37).

E. Composition Imagine that you are the police officer. Describe in about 100 words what you did from the time you saw the lights in Mr. Price's store until you told him about the problem. Do not introduce any ideas that are not included in the reading.

F. Look at this sentence:
Mr. Price *had iron bars fitted* to all the windows. Causing something to be done by someone else is expressed by the pattern *have* or *get* + noun phrase + past participle.

Now complete the following sentences, paying particular attention to the idea expressed by this pattern.

1. I'm going to have my eyes _____ (examine) tomorrow.
2. Your handwriting is difficult to read. You should have your letters _____ (type).
3. Those pants don't fit you. Why don't you get them _____ (alter)?
4. It's a shame she's had her hair _____ (dye).
5. I used to have this magazine _____ (send) to me while I worked overseas.
6. The tree in the front yard makes this room dark. We should get it _____ (cut down).
7. This room will look a lot better when we get the old fireplace _____ (take out) and a new one _____ (put in).
8. Leave those suitcases in the lobby and I'll have them _____ (send up) to your room later.
9. How much does it cost to have a suit _____ (clean)?
10. These are the pictures we had _____ (take) at the wedding.

SECTION TWO
RECALL EXERCISES

Verbs
Articles
epositions and Adverbial Particles
Linking Words

VERBS

Complete each of the following passages by supplying the correct form of the verb.

A.   That evening I _____ (go) _____ (have) dinner
with my aunt and uncle. They _____ also _____
(invite) a young woman so that there _____ (be) four
people at the table. Her face _____ (be) familiar. I
_____ (be) quite sure that we _____ (not, meet)
before, but I _____ (not, can) (remember) where I
_____ (see) her. In the course of conversation,
however, the young woman _____ (happen) _____
(mention) that she _____ (lose) her wallet that
afternoon. All at once I _____ (realize) where I
_____ (see) her. She _____ (be) the young girl in
the photograph, although she _____ (be) now much
older. She _____ (be) very surprised, of course, when I
_____ (be able) _____ (describe) her wallet to her.
Then I _____ (explain) that I _____ (recognize) her
from the photograph I _____ (find) in the wallet. My
uncle _____ (insist on) _____ (go) to the police
station immediately _____ (claim) the wallet.

(CP-2)

B.   The children _____ (stop) _____ (chatter) as
Miss Rios _____ (enter) the classroom. Then in a loud
chorus, they _____ (say), "Good morning, teacher."
      Miss Rios _____ (smile), _____ (say) good
morning and _____ (glance) quickly around the room.
There _____ (seem) _____ (be) about thirty-five in
the class—perhaps a few more girls than boys. All of the
children _____ (be) _____ (watch) her intently,
_____ (wait) no doubt _____ (find out) what sort of
person she _____ (be). "I _____ (suppose) you
_____ (want) _____ (know) my name," she
_____ (say).
      But before she _____ (can) _____ (tell) them,
someone in the class _____ (call out), "You _____
(be) Miss Rios." Everybody _____ (laugh). Miss Rios
_____ (laugh) too.

(CP-5)

C.   Lydia _____ (be) now quite sure that she _____ (be going) _____ (miss) her train, even though she _____ (be) not very far from the station. She _____ (be) _____ (wonder) what _____ (do) when a bus _____ (come along), heading in the direction of the station. The bus stop _____ (be) just at the next corner, so Lydia _____ (get) her suitcase out of the taxi and _____ (run) towards the bus, which _____ (stop) _____ (leave off) some passengers _____ . The bus driver _____ (see) her _____ (run) and _____ (wait) for her. Lydia _____ (get) to the station just in time and _____ (manage) _____ (catch) her train after all.

(CP-7)

D.   "I _____ (wish) he _____ (let) me _____ (know)," the young man _____ (say). "I _____ (write) him a letter _____ (say) that I _____ (be coming). Now I _____ (make) this long trip for nothing. Well, since he _____ (not, be) here, there _____ (be) no point in _____ (wait)."

He _____ (thank) Mrs. Crenshaw and _____ (go out). Mrs. Crenshaw _____ (go) to the window and _____ (watch) him _____ (drive off). As soon as his car _____ (be) out of sight, she _____ (call out), "You _____ (can) _____ (come out) now, Mr. Mancini. He _____ (go)."

Mr. Mancini _____ (come out of) the kitchen, where he _____ (be waiting).

"Thanks very much, Mrs. Crenshaw," he _____ (say), _____ (laugh). "You _____ (do) that very well. These nephews of mine never _____ (give) me any peace. That young man _____ (be) the worst of them all. As you _____ (see), when he _____ (need) money, he _____ (go) to great lengths _____ (find) me. Well, maybe next time he _____ (not, warn) me in advance by _____ (write) a letter!"

(CP-8)

E.   I _____ (be) delighted _____ (get) your letter this morning. I really should _____ (write) to you several

120

weeks ago — I _____ (owe) you a letter, I _____
(know) — but I _____ (be) terribly busy. The children
_____ (seem) _____ (take up) all of my time. Ann
_____ (be) five next month and I _____ (think) of
_____ (send) her to nursery school. Our little one
_____ just (start) _____ (walk) and _____ (not,
give) me a moment's peace. But you _____ (know)
what it _____ (be) like! How _____ (be) all your
children? They _____ (must) _____ (love) _____
(live) in the country!

I _____ (be) afraid we _____ (not, can) _____
(come) _____ (see) you next weekend, as you _____
(suggest). Tom's mother _____ (come) _____
(spend) the day with us on Sunday. What about the
weekend after this one — the 22nd and 23rd? We
_____ (be) free that weekend and _____ (love)
_____ (come). We _____ (be) anxious _____ (see)
your new house.

(CP-9)

F.   When I _____ (reach) the motel, I _____
(register) and _____ (go) straight to my room. Since I
_____ (be going) _____ (be) there for two full
weeks, I _____ (decide) _____ (unpack) my things
and _____ (get) _____ (settle) before _____ (go
out) _____ (eat). As soon as I _____ (empty) the
suitcases, I _____ (leave) my room and _____
(head) for the restaurant across the street. I _____
barely _____ (step) through the door of the restaurant
when an all too familiar voice _____ (greet) me. I
_____ (not, escape) from my tiresome next-door
neighbor after all! He _____ (grasp) me warmly by
the hand and _____ (insist) that we _____ (have)
dinner together.

"This _____ (be) a pleasant surprise," he _____
(say). "I never _____ (expect) _____ (see) you again
after all these years."

(CP-12)

G.   Fred _____ (open) his box and _____ (lay) the
books out on the counter.

"I _____ (not, pretend) _____ (know) much about old books," he _____ (say). "I _____ (have) these for years, and I _____ even _____ (not, read) them. My grandfather _____ (leave) them to me, as a matter of fact. But my wife _____ (be) always after me _____ (get rid of) them. She _____ (say) they _____ (be) just _____ (clutter up) our apartment. So I _____ (think) I _____ (bring) them in _____ (show) them to you, just in case they _____ (happen) _____ (be) worth something."

In the meantime, the man _____ (pick up) the books one by one and _____ (examine) them. He _____ (shake) his head.

"They _____ (not, be) worth very much," he _____ (say). "I _____ (can) _____ (give) you three or four dollars for them if you _____ (want) _____ (get rid of) them. I _____ (not, can) _____ (offer) you much more, I _____ (be) afraid."

(CP-13)

H. It _____ (be) dark in the attic, just as Miss Lee _____ (warn) him. Jim _____ (find) the small end windows and _____ (force) them open, _____ (let in) more light. He _____ (can) just _____ (make out) the boxes which Miss Lee _____ (tell) him about.

"When my father _____ (die)," Miss Lee _____ (say), "his large library _____ (be donated) to the University. Most of his papers and some other possessions of no great value _____ (be stored) in boxes and _____ (put) up in the attic. They _____ (be) there ever since. I _____ (not, suppose) anyone _____ (go) in there for over ten years."

"What about his diaries?" _____ (ask) Jim. "In one of his letters to a colleague, Dr. Lee _____ (mention) that he _____ (keep) a diary."

"I _____ (not, remember) _____ (see) any diaries," _____ (say) Miss Lee, with a puzzled look on her face. "Of course, he _____ (may) _____ (destroy) them before his last illness. Otherwise, they _____ (must) _____ (be) in one of those boxes in the attic."

(CP-15)

I.   At this point the man suddenly _____ *(let out)* a loud cry. Everyone _____ *(turn)* _____ *(see)* what _____ *(happen)*. The man _____ *(be)* _____ *(bend)* over his monkey, which now _____ *(be)* _____ *(lie)* stretched out on the sidewalk. He _____ *(pick up)* the lifeless body and, _____ *(hold)* it close to him, _____ *(begin)* _____ *(cry)*. A young man _____ *(step forward)* from the crowd, _____ *(take out)* his wallet and _____ *(drop)* several dollar bills into the hat. Jeff and several other people _____ *(follow)* the young man's example, and soon the hat _____ *(be)* _____ *(fill)* with coins and dollar bills. Meanwhile the man _____ *(continue)* _____ *(hold)* the dead monkey in his arms and _____ *(seem)* _____ *(be)* oblivious to what _____ *(be)* _____ *(go on)* around him.

(CP-17)

J.   "Now," _____ *(say)* Detective Travis, _____ *(pull up)* a chair close to the injured man's bed and _____ *(sit down)*. "I _____ *(hope)* you _____ *(feel)* well enough _____ *(answer)* a few questions."

"Yes, I _____ *(guess)* so," _____ *(say)* the man _____ *(lie)* in the bed. He _____ *(try)* _____ himself _____ *(raise up)* slightly, but the effort _____ *(seem)* too much for him. The nurse _____ *(place)* another pillow behind his head and _____ *(leave)* the room. "I _____ *(be back)* in just a few minutes," she _____ *(tell)* the detective.

"First of all," _____ *(say)* the detective, _____ *(open)* his memo pad, "we _____ *(have)* _____ *(establish)* your identity."

The man _____ *(look)* astonished. "My identity . . . ," he _____ *(say)* slowly. "_____ you even _____ *(not, know)* who I _____ *(be)*? How long _____ I _____ *(be)* _____ *(lie)* here like this?"

"Three days," the detective _____ *(tell)* him. "But we _____ *(find)* no identification of any kind on you. Whoever _____ *(beat up)* you _____ also _____ *(steal)* your wallet."

(CP-18)

K. One summer evening I _____ (be) _____ (sit) by the open window, _____ (read) a good science fiction book. I _____ (be) so engrossed in the story I _____ (be) _____ (read) that I _____ (not, notice) that it _____ (be) _____ (get) dark. When I _____ (realize) it _____ (be) too dark for me _____ (read) easily, I _____ (put) the book down and _____ (get up) _____ (turn on) a light. Just as I _____ (be) about _____ (close) the drapes, I _____ (hear) someone _____ (cry), "Help! Help!" It _____ (seem) _____ (come) from the trees at the other end of the yard. I _____ (look out) but it _____ (be) now too dark _____ (see) anything clearly. Almost immediately I _____ (hear) the cry again. It _____ (sound) like a child, but I _____ (not, can) _____ (imagine) what anybody _____ (will) _____ (be) _____ (do) in our backyard, unless one of the neighborhood children _____ (climb) a tree and _____ (not, be able) _____ (get down).

(CP-21)

L. Since this _____ (be) his first space flight, Joe _____ (be) nervous at first. But, once the launch _____ (be) successfully _____ (complete) and the ship _____ (achieve) the initial orbit around Earth, he _____ (relax) and _____ (sit back) _____ (enjoy) the flight. A few minutes later the Captain's voice _____ (come over) the speaker system. "Our present speed," he _____ (begin), "_____ (be) twenty-four thousand two hundred and fifty miles per hour, _____ (give) us an Earth orbit time of forty-seven minutes." Joe _____ (smile). He _____ (have) some idea now how the pioneer astronauts _____ (must) _____ (feel) a hundred years ago when they _____ (orbit) the earth for the first time. The Captain _____ (continue), "Our flight time _____ (be) nine months, two weeks, six days and seventeen hours. We _____ (be) _____ . . ." Suddenly Joe _____ (sit) upright in his seat. Something _____ (be) radically wrong. His total flight time, _____ (include) transit time on the moon, _____ (be) only _____ (suppose) _____ *(be)* seven days. He immediately _____ *(press)* the call button. When a flight attendant _____ *(appear)* at his side, he _____ *(say)*, "This _____ *(be)* the shuttle to the moon, _____ *(not, be)* it?" The attendant _____ *(look)* at him in surprise and _____ *(reply)*, "The Moon shuttle? Oh no, sir. This flight _____ *(go)* to Mars!"

(CP-24)

M. Phil _____ never _____ *(be)* to this part of the library before, and he _____ *(wonder)* why it _____ *(not, be)* _____ *(include)* in the tour for freshman students last week. He _____ *(reach)* in his pocket and _____ *(pull out)* a scrap of paper on which he _____ *(scribble)* the title and call number of the book he _____ *(be)* _____ *(suppose)* _____ *(read)*. Then he _____ *(walk around)* the room almost on tiptoe, afraid of _____ *(disturb)* the serious readers with his heavy shoes. The shelves _____ *(be)* filled with thick volumes: dictionaries in many languages, encyclopedias, atlases, biographies and other works. Off in one corner he finally _____ *(find)* the section he _____ *(be looking for)*. The books in this section _____ *(be)* on a high shelf out of his reach, but he _____ *(locate)* a small stepladder over by the encyclopedias and quietly _____ *(move)* it into position. Unfortunately, as he _____ *(be coming)* back down the ladder, the book he _____ *(take off)* the shelf _____ *(slip)* out of his hand and _____ *(fall)* to the floor with a loud crash. Everybody in the library _____ *(look up)* at him at the same time, obviously annoyed by the disturbance. Phil _____ *(feel)* his face _____ *(turn)* red as he _____ *(pick up)* his book, which luckily _____ *(not, seem)* _____ *(be)* _____ *(damage)* by the fall.

(CP-26)

N. By eleven o'clock Mr. Wood _____ *(feel)* very tired. He _____ *(be)* ready for bed but he _____ *(know)* from past experience that he _____ *(not, be going)* _____ *(be able)* _____ *(get)* to sleep. _____ *(put*

on) his pajamas, he _____ (prop up) himself _____
in bed with a book. He _____ (try) _____
(concentrate) on his book, but the noise from the room
directly above his head _____ (be) too much. He
_____ (find) himself _____ (read) the same page
over and over again. _____ (give up), he _____
(turn out) the light and _____ (bury) his head in the
pillows in a desperate effort _____ (shut out) the
noise. Finally, after what _____ (seem) like hours, he
_____ (switch on) the light back _____ and
_____ (look at) his watch. It _____ (be) a little after
three o'clock. He _____ (be) furious. _____ (throw
back) the covers, he _____ (jump) out of bed, _____
(put on) his robe and _____ (march) out of the
bedroom and across the living room to the front door of
his apartment. He _____ (jerk open) the door_____
and _____ (charge) out into the hallway, _____
(head for) the stairs.

O.   One Friday night when he _____ (count) his money
after _____ (close up), he _____ (find) that he
_____ (take in) nearly a thousand dollars that day.
This _____ (be) an exceptionally large sum of money
and the thought of _____ (keep) it in the store over
the weekend _____ (make) him very nervous. He
_____ (know) that it _____ (will) _____ (be)
better _____ (take) it over to his son's house where
there _____ (be) a small safe, but it _____ (be)
_____ (rain) hard that night and his son _____
(live) all the way on the other side of town. _____
(decide) _____ (not, venture) out in the rain, he
_____ (take) the money with him to his bedroom,
_____ (put) it in the pocket of his overcoat and
_____ (lock) the coat in the closet. He _____ (put)
the key to the closet under his pillow and _____ (go)
to bed.

(CP-30)

ARTICLES

Complete each of the following passages by supplying *a, an* or *the*.

A. When I was walking down _____ street _____ other day, I happened to notice _____ small brown leather wallet lying on _____ sidewalk. I picked it up and opened it to see if I could find out _____ owner's name. There was nothing inside it except some change and _____ old photograph — _____ picture of _____ woman and _____ young girl about twelve years old, who looked like _____ woman's daughter. I put _____ photograph back and took _____ wallet to _____ police station, where I handed it to _____ desk sergeant. Before I left, _____ sergeant took down my name and address in case _____ owner might want to write and thank me.

(CP-2)

B. First of all, there's Dr. Stone — my favorite, I must confess. He's _____ man of about sixty-five, with gray hair and _____ pleasant face. He gave up his medical practice _____ short time ago and is traveling around _____ world before he retires to Florida. As _____ young man, he served overseas for _____ number of years as _____ doctor in _____ Navy. He speaks several languages and has told us _____ lot about _____ port cities we're going to visit. He seems to have been everywhere. During _____ day, when he's not talking to other passengers (you get _____ impression he already knows everybody on board!), he sits on deck reading or looking out at sea through _____ old telescope.

(CP-3)

C. It was time to get started. "Now let me see," said Miss Rios, looking at her class schedule. " _____ first subject is English."

"Oh! Please read us _____ story," begged one of _____ girls.

127

Several of _____ children echoed this request. Miss Rios smiled.

"All right," she said. "But first of all, I want you to write _____ short letter to John Young. We'll send _____ letters to him in _____ hospital to cheer him up. Afterwards, I'll read you _____ story."

They were all writing and drawing busily when Miss Rios slipped out of _____ room to get _____ book she had left in _____ teachers' lounge. She passed _____ Principal in _____ hall.

"Any problems with that class?" _____ Principal asked.

"Not so far," said Miss Rios confidently. "They all seem very well behaved."

(CP-5)

D. Just then he noticed that her bottle of milk, which is always delivered early in _____ morning, was still on _____ porch. This worried him. If Mrs. Carter had not taken in her milk, maybe she was sick. Bill walked around _____ house until he found _____ open window. It was _____ small window, but he managed to squeeze through. He went into _____ hall. There he almost stumbled over Mrs. Carter, who was lying unconscious at _____ foot of _____ stairs. Realizing that he needed to get help, and knowing that there was no telephone there, he rushed out of _____ house, stopped _____ passing car and told _____ driver to go to _____ nearest telephone and call _____ ambulance.

(CP-6)

E. Just then _____ taxi came around _____ corner and moved slowly toward her. Lydia knew that _____ fare to _____ station was at least four dollars, which was more than she could afford; but she quickly made up her mind that it would be well worth _____ extra expense in order to be sure of catching her train. So she waved down _____ taxi and got in. She told _____ driver that she had to catch _____ two-thirty train.

128

He nodded and said that he would take _____
shortcut to get her to _____ station in time.

(CP-7)

F.   He was just in _____ middle of describing _____
terrifying experience he once had in _____ small
sailboat out on _____ ocean during _____ storm,
when there was _____ loud crash from _____
bedroom upstairs — _____ one where my brother and
I were going to sleep.

    "It sounds like _____ roof caved in!" exclaimed my
uncle, with _____ loud laugh.

    When we got to _____ top of _____ stairs and
opened _____ bedroom door, we could not see
anything at first because of _____ clouds of dust that
filled _____ room. When _____ dust began to
settle, we saw _____ strange sight. Part of _____
roof had fallen in and broken boards, shingles and huge
chunks of plaster had come down on my bed.

(CP-10)

G.   When he picked up _____ last book, however, his
expression changed and his eyes lighted up all of
_____ sudden.

    "What is it?" asked Fred.

    "Now this one *is* worth something!" exclaimed
_____ man, turning _____ pages carefully. "It's
_____ very rare edition."

    He handed _____ book to Fred, who looked at
_____ title. It was _____ novel by _____ author
that he had never heard of. Of all _____ books he had
packed up to bring in, this one had looked _____ least
interesting.

(CP-13)

H.   After searching through _____ number of drawers,
Miss Lee found _____ key to _____ attic.

    "It may not be light enough to see anything up there,"
she said as she handed him _____ key. "There are
small windows at each end of _____ attic, but I

suspect they'll be covered with dust and won't let much light in."

There were about _____ dozen boxes in all. Jim did not know where to begin. He opened first one, then _____ other, but did not find anything that looked like _____ diary. Then he decided to try _____ largest box. It was full of papers. As he began to sort through stacks of papers, _____ bundle of note pads tied together with string caught his eye. On _____ cover of _____ top one were scribbled _____ words, "Diary–1946-47."

(CP-15)

I. _____ small crowd had gathered near _____ entrance to _____ park. His curiosity aroused, Jeff crossed _____ street to see what was happening. He found that _____ center of attraction was _____ old man with _____ performing monkey. He soon discovered that _____ monkey's tricks were not spectacular so, after throwing _____ few coins into _____ hat which _____ man had placed on _____ sidewalk, Jeff began to move away, along with other members of _____ crowd.

(CP-17)

J. Once we stepped out on deck, we found out that one of _____ crew had seen _____ man in _____ ocean some distance from _____ ship. He had informed _____ captain, and _____ captain had ordered _____ ship to be turned around at once. We were now only about two hundred yards or so from _____ man, and _____ lifeboat had already been lowered into _____ water. In it there were four crewmembers, _____ officer and _____ ship's doctor. _____ officer shouted _____ order and _____ crew began to row away from _____ ship. Looking in _____ direction _____ lifeboat was heading, we were able to make out _____ exact position of _____ man in _____ water. He was holding on to some large object that might have been _____ broken section of _____ small fishing boat.

(CP-19)

K. I went into _____ restaurant, which was already crowded, and ordered _____ large bowl of clam chowder and my favorite seafood platter. While I was waiting for _____ chowder to arrive, I looked around _____ restaurant to see if there was anyone I knew. It was then that I noticed that _____ man sitting at _____ corner table near _____ door kept glancing in my direction, as if he knew me. I certainly did not know him, however. _____ man had _____ newspaper open in front of him, which he was pretending to read, but I could see that he was keeping _____ eye on me. When _____ waiter brought my clam chowder, _____ man was clearly puzzled by _____ familiar way in which _____ waiter and I chatted with each other. He seemed even more puzzled as time went on and it became obvious that all of _____ waiters in _____ restaurant knew me. Eventually he got up and went into _____ kitchen. After _____ few minutes he came out again, paid his bill and left without another glance in my direction.

(CP-20)

L. John opened _____ door and surveyed _____ office in one quick glance. It was _____ large, tastefully decorated room with comfortable-looking furniture arranged more like _____ living room than _____ office, which was all-important, he realized, in creating _____ kind of friendly and relaxed atmosphere that makes clients instantly feel at home. Over on one side was _____ receptionist's desk and beyond that, covering _____ whole back area, were rows of desks for _____ sales staff. As he walked up to _____ receptionist's desk, he could not help but wonder which of _____ desks he would be assigned to. "You're early for your appointment," _____ receptionist said after he identified himself. "Mr. Becker hasn't arrived yet, but you can have _____ seat over there and wait for him," she told him, pointing to _____ first desk in _____ third row. "Mr. Becker said that one will be yours."

(CP-23)

M. In _____ meantime, my brother's flight had arrived and, after getting his suitcases, we headed for my car in _____ parking lot. During _____ drive home I had plenty of time to tell him all about my unfortunate experience. When we got home and were unloading _____ car, I could hardly believe my eyes when my brother brought _____ briefcase out of _____ car, which he had found on _____ floor in _____ back seat. It was _____ briefcase I thought I had lost, but which obviously I had never taken into _____ airport in _____ first place! I realized that at that moment _____ airline people were painstakingly checking each piece of luggage on their Denver, St. Louis and Chicago flights, looking for my briefcase, and I dreaded _____ thought of having to call them and tell them I had found it in my car.

(CP-25)

N. Henry tried to calm his nerves by examining Mr. Foster's office in detail. On his right there was _____ large window with _____ view of _____ factory yard. Henry could see two men on _____ forklift moving across _____ yard toward what seemed to be _____ large warehouse. Close to _____ window there were three chairs arranged around one end of _____ long conference table, with _____ pitcher of water and some glasses on _____ table. To Henry's left there were bookshelves covering _____ whole wall from floor to ceiling. _____ shelves were empty except for _____ dozen or so books, _____ pile of technical journals, which looked as if they might topple off _____ shelf at any moment, and _____ plastic duck standing by itself on _____ top shelf and looking _____ bit out of place in _____ executive's office. Henry could not help wondering how it got there.

(CP-28)

O. Mr. Price, _____ owner of _____ antique store in Daly City, lived alone in _____ small apartment above his store. Because of _____ many valuable articles he kept on _____ premises, he was always afraid that one night somebody might break into his store. Years before, when he had first opened his small shop there, he had iron bars fitted to all _____ windows and double locks put on all _____ doors. As _____ added safety measure, he had special cabinets built so that he could lock up his most valuable objects every night. But in spite of these precautions, he never felt safe, especially when he had _____ lot of money in _____ store after _____ good day's business.

(CP-30)

PREPOSITIONS AND ADVERBIAL PARTICLES

Complete each of the following passages by supplying the correct preposition or adverbial particle.

A.   It was already late when we started _____ _____ the next town, which _____ _____ the map was about fifteen miles away _____ the other side _____ the hills. We felt sure that we would find a place to spend the night there. Darkness fell soon after we left, but luckily there were no other cars _____ the road as we drove quickly _____ the narrow winding road that led _____ the hills. As we climbed higher, it became colder and heavy rain began to fall, making it difficult _____ times to see the road clearly. I asked John to slow _____ .

After traveling _____ about twenty miles, there was still no sign _____ the town which was marked _____ the map. We were beginning to get worried. Then, _____ warning, the car stopped. We had run _____ _____ gas. Although we had very little to eat _____ us, only a few cookies and some candy bars, we decided to spend the night _____ the car.

(CP-1)

B.   Then there's a man I don't like very much, a construction engineer _____ the name _____

Barlow. He's been _____ leave _____ California
and is now _____ his way back _____ the job he has
_____ Singapore. He's very athletic and spends most
_____ his time swimming or playing tennis. I've
never _____ my life met a man _____ such a loud
laugh. He has the cabin _____ _____ mine and I
can hear him laugh even _____ the thick cabin walls!

The other person who sits _____ our table is Mrs.
Lang. I haven't found _____ very much _____ her
yet. She's quiet and doesn't talk very much, except to
consult _____ the doctor _____ her children's
various ailments. She's _____ her way to join her
husband _____ Bangkok.

(CP-3)

C.   Dawn was just breaking as they climbed _____ the
boat and pushed _____ _____ the bank. A swift
current carried them downstream, so there was no need
to row. They took turns keeping the boat _____ the
middle _____ the river. Three hours later they
entered the woods where they intended to spend the next
few days.

"Let's go ashore now and fix some lunch," suggested
Frank. "This looks like a good spot."

While Frank tied _____ the boat, the other two
boys started gathering wood _____ a fire. When they
came _____, each _____ a little kindling and an
armload _____ wood, they found Frank looking very
worried.

(CP-4)

D.   A car pulled _____ _____ the Driftwood Motel
and a young man got _____. Pausing only _____
an instant to make sure that he had come _____ the
right place, he went _____ the motel office and rang
the bell _____ the counter to attract somebody's
attention.

Mrs. Crenshaw, the motel manager, who was busy
_____ the kitchen _____ that moment, hurried
_____, wiping her hands _____ a towel. The young
man raised his hat.

"Excuse me," he said. "I'm looking _____ my uncle, Mr. Mancini. I believe he's staying here."

"He *was* staying here," Mrs. Crenshaw corrected him. "But I'm afraid that he went _____ _____ San Francisco yesterday."

"Oh, no!" said the young man, looking disappointed. "I understood that he was going to be here _____ the end _____ the month. At least that's what they told me when I called his office."

(CP-8)

E.   Mrs. Winters was tired _____ a day _____ shopping, so she went _____ a coffee shop to have some coffee and to rest _____ a few minutes _____ going back _____ the hotel where she and her husband were staying. While she was sitting _____ the counter sipping her coffee, she suddenly remembered that she had to buy some cough medicine _____ her husband.

"Is there a drugstore _____ here?" she asked the man _____ the counter.

"Yes, ma'am," the man said. "There's one about three blocks _____ here. Turn right when you go _____ the door, then go to the second intersection and turn left. You'll see the drugstore _____ the end _____ the block _____ the right-hand side. It closes _____ five, but if you hurry, you'll get there _____ time."

Mrs. Winters followed the directions carefully and found the drugstore _____ any difficulty. She bought the cough medicine and started to make her way _____ _____ the coffee shop. But after she had walked _____ about ten minutes and there was still no sign _____ the coffee shop, she realized that she must have made a mistake.

(CP-11)

F.   Then one _____ the men looked _____ his watch, clapped his hands and said something _____ the others. Quickly they all went _____ their desks and, _____ a matter _____ seconds, everyone was hard _____ work. No one paid any attention _____

Marie. Finally she went _____ _____ the man who
was sitting _____ the desk nearest the door and
explained that this was her first day _____ the office.
Hardly looking _____ _____ his work, he told her
to have a seat and wait _____ Mr. King, who would
arrive _____ any moment. Then Marie realized that
the day's work _____ the office began just before Mr.
King arrived. Later she found _____ that he lived
_____ Connecticut and came _____ Manhattan
_____ the same train every morning, arriving
_____ the office promptly _____ 9:35, so that his
staff knew exactly when to start working.

(CP-14)

G.   Thank you _____ your letter _____ November
7th, which I am answering _____ behalf _____ my
husband. Apparently you have not heard that about a
month ago my husband was taken seriously ill.
Although he is much better now, the doctor has ordered
him to take a complete rest _____ _____ least
three months. As a matter _____ fact, we are leaving
_____ Hawaii just as soon as he is able to travel and
we will probably not return _____ _____ the
middle _____ February.
_____ view _____ this, I regret that my husband
is unable to accept your kind invitation _____ the
dinner which you are having _____ December 1st. He
has asked me, however, to send his best wishes and
congratulations _____ you _____ your fifth
anniversary, and to say that he hopes to see you again
_____ the spring.

(CP-16)

H.   "You were attacked _____ someone and your car
was stolen too," the detective explained patiently. "So
you see, we've been completely _____ the dark. We
haven't had much to work _____. You were found
Tuesday night lying unconscious _____ a parking lot
_____ the New Moon Restaurant, where you had
stopped _____ dinner that evening. That's all we

136

know _____ you. Anyway, maybe now you can tell us who you are and what happened _____ you last Tuesday night."

The man raised his right hand _____ his bandaged head and said slowly, "I . . . I'm not sure . . . what happened . . ."

"We think somebody attacked you when you were getting _____ your car," the detective continued. "They were probably watching you when you came _____ _____ the restaurant. Then when you unlocked your car and started to get _____, they sneaked _____ _____ you. You received a very heavy blow _____ the head. Can't you remember anything that happened?"

(CP-18)

I.   When I had finished and was about to pay my bill, I called the owner _____ the restaurant and asked him what the man had wanted. The owner seemed a little embarrassed _____ my question and _____ first did not want to tell me. I insisted. "Well," he said, "that man was a detective." "Really?" I said, showing my surprise. "He was certainly very interested _____ me. But why?" "He followed you here because he thought you were the man he was looking _____," the owner _____ the restaurant said. "When he came _____ the kitchen, he showed me a photograph _____ the wanted man. I must say he looked very much like you! _____ course, since we know you here, I was able to convince him that he had made a mistake." "It's lucky I came _____ a restaurant where I'm known," I said. "Otherwise, I might have been arrested."

(CP-20)

J.   I am not sure that you will remember me, but we met _____ Bethany last year. It was _____ your daughter's wedding. Her husband David is an old friend _____ mine (_____ fact, we were roommates _____ college), and I came _____ New York _____ the wedding. You and I had a long chat _____ the reception and I told you a little _____ my

137

job as a reporter _____ the *New York Times*. You said
that I should get _____ touch _____ you if I ever
decided to come back _____ Bethany.

_____ that time I had every intention _____
staying _____ New York, but since then I have
changed my mind and now I would like very much to get
a job back _____ my own hometown. My problem is
this—I have been _____ now _____ so long (since
1967, _____ fact) that I have no job contacts _____
Bethany. That is why I am writing _____ you now. I
would appreciate it very much if you could put me
_____ touch _____ anyone who could help me or
advise me. I hesitated writing _____ you like this, but
any suggestions you might have would be appreciated.
My best wishes _____ you and Mrs. Anderson.

(CP-22)

K. _____ a quick breakfast _____ the coffee shop
_____ _____ the hotel, John crossed the street and
walked directly _____ the Becker Real Estate office.
As he approached the glass-front office, he saw his
reflection and paused to straighten his shirt collar and
adjust his tie, pretending to be looking _____ the
large display _____ photographs visible _____ the
glass. They were photographs _____ houses _____
sale and _____ each one was a small placard _____
a brief description _____ the property and the price. It
was an excellent location _____ the office, he thought,
and the display could not help but attract the attention
_____ people passing _____ there every day.
Pausing _____ the door, he glanced _____ his
watch. His appointment _____ Mr. Becker was
_____ nine-fifteen, which was still another ten
minutes, but he did not want to run the risk _____
being late the first day.

(CP-23)

L. Joe was looking forward _____ his first trip
_____ *Thunderbolt*, as the space shuttle _____ the
moon was called. He had heard a great deal _____ the

trip _____ his friends who had already been _____
the shuttle. They all advised him to go _____ the
winter, not _____ the summer. But Joe is the kind
_____ person who listens _____ everybody's advice
and then does exactly what he had planned to do
_____ the first place.

Joe entered the space station shortly _____ three
o'clock _____ a Friday afternoon _____ the middle
_____ July. This was a particularly bad time to take a
flight because all _____ the month _____ July,
guided tours _____ schoolchildren _____ all
_____ the United States flood _____ Cape Ortega
to take advantage _____ the special summer discount
rates _____ students. He had to join one _____ the
long lines _____ young students who were waiting
their turn _____ the preflight examination. When
Joe's turn came to step _____ _____ the
computerized panel, he had a difficult time figuring
_____ how the controls _____ the analyzer worked
and how to get the door _____ the analyzer chamber
to open so that he could step _____. The people
_____ the long line _____ him began to grumble
impatiently _____ the delay, but he finally completed
the examination sequence and received the printout
_____ the results _____ a blue data card. The card
verified that he was approved _____ space travel.

(CP-24)

M. He had just sat _____ _____ one _____ the
tables when he found the young library assistant
standing _____ _____ him. "You must be more
careful handling these books," she whispered softly.
Satisfied that she had done her duty, she turned to go
back _____ her desk. Phil opened his book and started
to leaf _____ it. Then he stopped and looked closely
_____ one _____ the pages. It was _____ Latin!
Somehow he had managed to get the wrong book. "Oh
no!" he blurted _____ _____ thinking. His voice
shattered the silence _____ the room and all _____
a sudden everyone was glaring _____ him. He winced
as he realized what he had done. Glancing quickly

_____ the room, he tried to make a silent apology, forming the words "I'm sorry" _____ his lips.

(CP-26)

N. Mr. Foster motioned _____ the chair _____ the other side _____ the desk and told Henry to take a seat. "I'm waiting _____ a call _____ Atlanta," he explained. The telephone rang just as he spoke. He picked _____ the receiver and spoke rapidly and impatiently _____ the telephone. Henry, meanwhile, was tense and nervous. _____ days he had dreaded the thought _____ this interview and now he wanted to get it over _____ as soon as possible. Having to wait like this just prolonged the agony. When Mr. Foster finished, his secretary came _____ _____ a big stack _____ letters. "I really won't keep you waiting much longer," said Mr. Foster apologetically, as he picked _____ the first letter and began to read it. "But these have to go _____ right away."

(CP-28)

O. Gasping _____ breath _____ running _____ the stairs, Mr. Wood positioned himself _____ his neighbor's door and knocked several times as loud as he could. But no one opened the door. This did not improve his temper. So he pounded _____ the door and shouted, "Open _____ _____ there!" A moment later the door opened and his neighbor, dressed _____ pajamas and rubbing his eyes, appeared _____ the doorway. Recognizing Mr. Wood and sensing that something terrible had happened, he asked, "What is it, Mr. Wood? What's the matter? Is the place _____ fire or something?" "No!" shouted Mr. Wood. "It's all this noise! How do you expect people to get any sleep?" His neighbor looked surprised and said, "What noise?" Mr. Wood stopped and listened _____ a moment. There was silence. He turned _____ slowly and looked _____ and _____ the empty hallway, and then turned _____ and leaned his head _____ the open doorway. "Where are all your guests?" he asked _____ a puzzled look _____ his face.

(CP-29)

LINKING WORDS

Complete each of the following passages by supplying the correct linking word.

A.   Our "meal" was soon over. I settled down to go to sleep, _____ John was restless _____ after a few minutes he got out of the car _____ went for a walk up the hill. Soon he came running back. From the top of the hill, he had seen the lights of the town we were looking for. We quickly unloaded everything we could from the car, including our heavy suitcases _____, with a great deal of effort, managed to push the car to the top of the hill. _____ we went back for our baggage, loaded the car again _____ started coasting down the hill. In less than fifteen minutes, we were in the town, _____ we found a hotel quite easily.

(CP-1)

B.   Dawn was just breaking _____ they climbed into the boat _____ pushed off from the bank. A swift current carried them downstream, _____ there was no need to row. They took turns keeping the boat towards the middle of the river. Three hours later they entered the woods _____ they intended to spend the next few days.
   "Let's go ashore now _____ fix some lunch," suggested Frank. "This looks like a good spot."
   _____ Frank tied up the boat, the other two boys started gathering wood for a fire. _____ they came back, each with a little kindling _____ an armload of wood, they found Frank looking very worried.

(CP-4)

C.   _____ Bill got to Mrs. Carter's house, he was surprised not to find her working in the yard. She usually spent her afternoons there _____ the weather was good. Bill went around to the back of the house, thinking _____ she might be in the kitchen. The door was locked _____ the curtains were drawn. Puzzled,

he returned to the front of the house _____ knocked
loudly on the front door. There was no answer. Bill
thought _____ this was very strange _____ he
knew _____ Mrs. Carter rarely left the house.

(CP-6)

D.   In November of last year, my brother _____ I were
invited to spend a few days with an uncle _____ had
just returned from overseas. He had a cabin in the
mountains, _____ he seldom spent much time there.
We understood the reason for this after our arrival. The
cabin had no comfortable furniture in it, several of the
windows were broken _____ the roof leaked—making
the whole place damp _____ uninviting.

On our first evening, we sat around the fire after supper listening to stories our uncle had to tell of his many
adventures overseas. I was so tired after the long trip
_____ I would have preferred to go to bed, _____ I
did not want to miss any of my uncle's exciting stories.

(CP-10)

E.   _____ the train neared the resort town on the coast
_____ I was going to spend my two-week vacation, I
got up from my seat _____ wandered up the aisle to
stretch my legs for a few minutes. At the front end of the
car, I stopped _____ exchanged a few words with one
of the passengers _____ I had met earlier in the
station. He had bought me a cup of coffee then.

_____ I turned to go back to my seat, I happened to
glance down the aisle _____ sitting just a few rows
back was a man _____ had lived next door to me
several years before. He was an incessant talker, I
remembered, _____ it used to take hours to get away
from him once he started a conversation. I was not at all
sorry _____ he moved away from our neighborhood.
We had not seen each other since then, _____ I
certainly did not want to spoil my vacation by renewing
an acquaintance with him now.

(CP-12)

F. _____ she finally reached the office marked "King Enterprises," she knocked on the door nervously _____ waited. There was no answer. She tapped on the door again, _____ still there was no reply. From inside the next office, she could hear the sound of voices, _____ she opened the door _____ went in.

_____ she was sure it was the same office she had been in two weeks before _____ she had had the interview with Mr. King, it looked quite different now. In fact, it hardly looked like an office at all. The employees were just standing around chatting _____ smoking. At the far end of the room, somebody must have just told a good joke, she concluded, _____ there was a loud burst of laughter _____ she came in. For a moment she had thought they were laughing at her.

(CP-14)

G. We first became aware that something unusual was happening _____ one of the ship's officers came up to the Chief Engineer _____ was sitting at our table, _____ spoke to him in a low voice. The Chief Engineer got up from the table immediately _____ with a brief excuse, _____ told us nothing, left the dining room. At first we thought _____ there had been an accident _____ _____ a fire had broken out on board, _____ in a few minutes word went around _____ a man had been seen floating in the ocean. We noticed _____ the ship was slowing down, _____ _____, with a sudden violent motion, it began to turn around. Some of the passengers did not wait to finish their meal _____ immediately rushed up on deck.

(CP-19)

H. One summer evening I was sitting by the open window, reading a good science fiction book. I was so engrossed in the story I was reading _____ I did not notice _____ it was getting dark. _____ I realized it was too dark for me to read easily, I put the book down _____ got up to turn on a light. Just as I was about to close the drapes, I heard someone crying, "Help! Help!"

It seemed to come from the trees at the other end of the yard. I looked out _____ it was now too dark to see anything clearly. Almost immediately I heard the cry again. It sounded like a child, _____ I could not imagine _____ anybody would be doing in our backyard, _____ one of the neighborhood children had climbed a tree _____ had not been able to get down.

(CP-21)

I. _____ I got to the airport, I discovered _____ the plane from Chicago _____ my brother was traveling on, had been delayed in Denver _____ of engine trouble _____ was expected to be about an hour late. Usually _____ I have to wait around the airport to meet a flight, I go to the observation deck _____ pass the time by watching planes land _____ take off, _____ that particular evening I had a splitting headache, _____ I thought the noise of jet engines might make worse. _____, I decided to walk around inside the terminal for a while.

_____ I was walking by the shops on the lower level, I happened to see a display of flight bags, _____ somehow reminded me all of a sudden of my briefcase _____ I realized _____ I was not carrying it now.

(CP-25)

SECTION THREE
AURAL COMPREHENSION TESTS

Aural Comprehension Passages
Dictation Passages

AURAL COMPREHENSION PASSAGES

A. Last year three friends of mine decided to spend their
vacation in the mountains. They set out in their car early in
the morning, and by late afternoon they had almost reached
the small town where they were going to stay. After
stopping for a cup of coffee at a roadside cafe, they drove off   5
again along the winding road that led to the mountains.
They had a map with them and, according to this, the town
they were going to stay in was only about fifteen miles away.

It soon got dark, and it began to rain — which of course
made it more difficult to see the road clearly. After they had   10
driven for about fifteen miles, there was still no sign of the
town. Obviously the map they had was not a very good one.

They went on for another five miles and, suddenly, the car
stopped. At first my friend thought they had run out of gas.
After checking, however, they found that this was not the   15
trouble. Something else had gone wrong with the car. Since
they could not start the engine again, they decided to spend
the night in the car, even though they had very little food
with them and there was not much room for three people.

It was early morning when another car finally came   20
along. They stopped the driver and asked him where the
town was. He told them that it was just on the other side of
the hill. They hitched their car to his, and he pulled them to
the top of the hill. After that their car ran all the way
downhill to the town, where they found a hotel and had a   25
good breakfast. Of course, if they had simply walked up the
hill the night before, they would not have had to spend an
uncomfortable night in the car.

(After CP-1)

A. Say whether the following statements are true or false.
1. They drove all day without stopping, until the car
broke down.
2. They forgot to take a map with them.
3. Their car did not stop because it had run out of gas.
4. They spent a comfortable night in the car.
5. They had to push their car to the top of the hill.

B. Answer the following questions.
1. Where were they going to spend their vacation?

2. Why was it difficult to see the road?
3. What did they ask the driver of the passing car?
4. What did the driver tell them?
5. What was the first thing they did when they reached the small town where they were going to stay?

B. One cold winter afternoon, the mailman was slowly pushing his mail cart up the hill that led out of the small town of Lance. He was walking very carefully because there was a lot of ice on the ground. He had only one more letter to deliver, and this was for an elderly lady who lived at the top   5 of Lance Hill. Everybody called her "Grandma."

She had lived alone ever since her daughter had moved to Hawaii many years before. She always used to invite the mailman in for coffee whenever he brought her a letter, and she would tell him about her two grandchildren in Hawaii,   10 whom she had never seen; however, she had lots of pictures of them, which she used to show him.

Just as the mailman approached her gate, a small boy came running down the hill. Suddenly the boy slipped on the icy street and fell. The mailman let his mail cart fall and   15 hurried across the street to help the boy. After a quick look, he saw that the boy had hurt his leg very badly. In fact, he thought the boy's leg might be broken. He knew that "Grandma" did not have a telephone, so he stopped a passing driver and asked him to take the boy to Lance Hospital.   20

(After CP-6)

A. Say whether the following statements are true or false.
1. The mailman had almost finished his day's work.
2. "Grandma's" daughter was taking a vacation in Hawaii.
3. Her grandchildren often came to see her.
4. The mailman soon found that the boy had hurt his leg.
5. The mailman used "Grandma's" telephone to call Lance Hospital.

B. Answer the following questions.
1. Why was the mailman walking up the hill carefully?
2. Where did "Grandma" live?

3. How many grandchildren did she have?
4. What did the mailman do when the boy fell?
5. Why did the mailman stop a passing driver?

C. Last January a friend of mine returned to San Francisco
after working in Senegal for two years as a Peace Corps
volunteer. He decided to live in the mountains where he
bought himself a small cabin. The cabin was in fairly good
condition, except for the roof, which leaked badly when it   5
rained hard. But my friend, who liked adventure in his life,
did not seem to mind that.

Not long after he had moved in, one of his old friends from
college came down to visit him, without even sending a
letter to warn him that he was coming. As the college pal   10
drove up to the cabin, my friend saw the car from the
kitchen window, and wondered for a moment if he should
pretend to be out. He had a good idea what his friend
wanted. He was going to try to borrow some money.

Even though the cabin was not very comfortable, my   15
friend's college pal announced he wanted to stay for two or
three days. As they sat by the fire after dinner, my friend
told his guest about some of his exciting adventures in
Senegal. He was just in the middle of one of his stories when
there was a tremendous crash upstairs. They both rushed up   20
to the bedroom. A strange sight met their eyes: part of the
ceiling had collapsed, falling right onto the bed where the
guest was going to sleep.

After that, the college pal did not even want to stay the
night, but my friend convinced him that it was safe to sleep   25
downstairs. The guest went back to San Francisco in the
morning, however, saying that he had to visit a sick brother.

(After CP-10)

A. **Say whether the following statements are true or false.**
   1. There was nothing wrong with the cabin except that
      the roof leaked.
   2. The writer's friend knew that his college pal was
      coming to visit him.
   3. He knew that his college friend wanted to borrow
      money.

4. They did not go to bed immediately after dinner.
5. The college pal enjoyed having exciting adventures.

B. *Answer the following questions.*
1. What was the writer's friend doing before he returned to San Francisco?
2. Where was the writer's friend when he saw his college pal's car drive up?
3. What were the friends doing when they heard the tremendous crash?
4. What did they discover when they opened the bedroom door?
5. What excuse did the college pal use for going back to San Francisco the following morning?

D. One day Mr. and Mrs. Medina went up to Boston to do some shopping. Even though they did not buy very much in the end, they had a busy day. By about four o'clock, they were both looking forward to having a snack. They found a restaurant but, just before they went in, Mrs. Medina   5
remembered that she had to buy some medicine for their son, who had a bad cough.

While she was in the drugstore, her husband noticed a bookstore on the other side of the street. He went across to have a look in the window. There he saw a copy of a novel   10
written by an author who was famous during the last century. He had always been very interested in this writer, so he went in and bought the book. His wife was waiting for him when he came out. He showed her the book, but she did not look at all pleased. She always complained that the old   15
books he bought only cluttered up the house.

After their snack, they caught the train back to Cape Cod where they lived. To their great surprise, an ex-neighbor of theirs, whom they had not seen for years, took a seat immediately across from them. They were both happy to see   20
him after all those years but, as they soon remembered, he was extremely talkative. If he got the chance, he would talk for hours. He happened to notice the book which Mr. Medina had bought, and he picked it up to leaf through it. As he opened the book, his eyes lighted up. He asked Mr. Medina   25
how much he had paid for it. When he found out that the book had cost only a few dollars, he told Medina that he had

been very lucky. The book happened to be a rare edition and was certainly worth over fifty dollars.

(After CP-13)

A. Say whether the following statements are true or false.
1. Mr. and Mrs. Medina bought a lot of things in Boston.
2. Mrs. Medina did not like her husband to buy old books.
3. They were sitting in the same car as their neighbor.
4. Mr. Medina told the ex-neighbor that he had bought a rare edition of a famous book.
5. The book was worth much more than Mr. Medina had paid for it.

B. Answer the following questions.
1. Why did Mrs. Medina go to the drugstore?
2. What did Mr. Medina do while his wife was at the drugstore?
3. Why didn't Mrs. Medina like old books?
4. What did they remember about their ex-neighbor?
5. Why did the ex-neighbor say that Mr. Medina had been lucky?

E. It was Monday morning. Susie left home early that day because she was going to start a new job in downtown Manhattan. She was only eighteen and this was her first job. When she got to the bus stop, there were so many people waiting that she almost called a passing taxi. Later she was   5
glad that she had waited for the bus because the traffic was so heavy that even a taxi would not have arrived much earlier. As it was, she was only a few minutes late.

She took the elevator to the eighth floor and went directly to the office where she had been interviewed by Mr. Samson   10
two weeks before. This was the man she was going to work for. She knocked lightly on the door and waited, but there was no answer. Just then she heard the sound of someone's voice coming from the next office. She opened the door and looked in. There was Mr. Samson — speaking angrily to all   15
the people in the office. He suddenly turned around and left the room.

Later in the day, Susie found out what had happened. Because Mr. Samson lived forty miles away in Westchester

County, he had to take the train to work, and would normally arrive at the office around nine-thirty. This morning, however, he happened to catch an earlier train and, when he arrived at the office, not a single person was working. They were all standing around — smoking, chatting and telling jokes.

(After CP-14)

A. *Say whether the following statements are true or false.*
 1. Susie had to take a taxi to the office.
 2. There was a lot of traffic that morning.
 3. There was somebody in Mr. Samson's office.
 4. Mr. Samson did not live in Manhattan.
 5. Mr. Samson had arrived early that morning.

B. *Answer the following questions.*
 1. Why was Susie glad that she had not taken the taxi?
 2. Who was Mr. Samson?
 3. Why did Susie open the door of the next office?
 4. What time did Mr. Samson usually arrive?
 5. What did Mr. Samson see when he arrived that morning?

F. I went to a meeting of the Clean Environment Agency last night. We had a very interesting speaker by the name of Fenton, who has written several books. He is in fact the person who was invited to address the agency on the occasion of our fifth anniversary, but unfortunately he was recovering from an illness at the time. He had been overworking and, as a result, his doctor ordered him to take a complete rest for at least three months.

He has since recovered, however, and last night he told us about his recent work. It is a book about the famous university professor Dr. Lee, who had studied solar energy in Germany until the first weeks of World War II. Fenton said that he had been planning to write a book about Dr. Lee for years. But, apart from a collection of letters and notes which the family had provided him with, he did not have much material.

Then one day he got a letter from one of Dr. Lee's colleagues, saying that the professor had kept a diary. Fenton immediately went to see Lee's niece to ask about it. She was not aware that her uncle had kept a diary, but she suggested that he contact Dr. Lee's daughter who was living in the old house right outside of town.

Fenton had sent Jim, one of his assistants, to talk to Miss Lee. Jim told her that *he* was writing a book about her father, so she went to the trouble of searching the entire house for the key to the attic where his papers had been stored. With the help of the diary that Jim found, Fenton was able to complete the biography.

(After CP-16)

A. Say whether the following statements are true or false.
1. Fenton had not been able to address the Clean Environment Agency on the occasion of its fifth anniversary.
2. Fenton had been ill because he worked too hard.
3. Dr. Lee's family had given enough material to write an account of the professor's life.
4. Dr. Lee's niece knew where her uncle's diaries were.
5. It was easy for Miss Lee to find the key to the attic.

B. Answer the following questions.
1. Why wasn't Mr. Fenton able to address the Clean Environment Agency on the occasion of their fifth anniversary?
2. Who was Dr. Lee?
3. How did Fenton come to hear about Dr. Lee's diaries?
4. How did Miss Lee find the key to the attic?
5. How did the diaries that Jim found help Fenton?

G. Detective Travis had been completely in the dark for three days. A man had been found unconscious in the parking lot behind the New Moon Restaurant. He had been robbed and his car had been stolen. The police had no idea of his identity until the man was finally able to tell them who he was and what had happened. He was also able to give them a description of the man, which the police sent to all the newspapers.

The next day Detective Travis got a message saying that
the man had been seen in a small town by the ocean. The   10
detective went there immediately. When he reached the
police station, the officer in charge had a second message for
him. The owner of a coffee shop at the beach had just called
him. According to him, a person matching the description in
the newspaper was having dinner in his restaurant.   15

The police rushed to the coffee shop. Two police officers
stationed themselves outside the front entrance, while
Detective Travis and another policeman entered through
the kitchen. Very excited, the owner of the restaurant
showed the officers the man he had been watching. He was   20
sitting at a corner table, reading a newspaper. Without a
doubt it was the right man.

Detective Travis did not want to disturb the other
customers, so he let the man finish his meal. Then, as the
man left the coffee shop, he was followed by two officers and 25
then arrested.

(After CP-20)

A. *Say whether the following statements are true or false.*
   1. At first, the police had no idea who the unconscious
      man was.
   2. The wanted man was spotted soon after the crime.
   3. All four police officers went into the restaurant.
   4. Detective Travis had a look at the man before he
      arrested him.
   5. Detective Travis arrested the man while he was in the
      restaurant.

B. *Answer the following questions.*
   1. What had happened to the man in the parking lot?
   2. How was the injured man able to help the police?
   3. Why did the owner of the restaurant call the police?
   4. What was the man doing when Detective Travis saw
      him?
   5. Why did Detective Travis let the man finish his meal?

H. After being away for several years, it is a strange
experience to return to the place where you were born and

raised. This happened to me a few months ago when I decided to come back to Bethany to take the job of chief reporter for the local newspaper here. 5

I got the job through the father-in-law of my former college roommate. I had met him at my friend's wedding. When I finally decided to come back to Bethany, mainly because I was tired of living in New York City, I wrote to him hoping that he might be able to put me in touch with 10 the right people. By a strange coincidence, he knew that the editor of the local newspaper wanted a reporter. As it turned out, I was just the right person for the job because I had had wide experience as a big-city reporter; in addition, I knew a great deal about Bethany. 15

This was not entirely true. When I came down to look for a place to live, I soon discovered that I did not know that much about the town. Many parts of it had completely changed. Having to look for an apartment, however, helped me rediscover Bethany because I had to look everywhere before 20 I found what I wanted.

In the end, I found the perfect place: an apartment in a one-story building on a quiet street. It faces a park, and from the beginning, I have felt right at home. And since the rent is so reasonable, I took the apartment without a moment's 25 hesitation.

(After CP-23)

A. Say whether the following statements are true or false.

1. The writer had not lived in Bethany for a long time.
2. He went back to work for the father of his college roommate.
3. He found that he still knew Bethany well.
4. It was not easy for him to find somewhere to live.
5. The apartment he found was expensive.

B. Answer the following questions.

1. What job did the writer take when he went back to Bethany?
2. Where had he met his friend's father-in-law?
3. Why was he the right person for the job?
4. How did he get to know Bethany again?
5. What were the things that he liked about the apartment?

I. While Joe was on a vacation on Mars, he radioed a friend of his who was living in Hong Kong, and asked if he could meet him at the space station in Los Angeles. The friend radioed back to say that he would be there. So when Joe reached the station, he was somewhat surprised to find that   5
his friend had not turned up.

He walked around for a little while and then, because he had a slight headache, he went into the space bar and had three energizing pills. He felt much better after that. He bought a couple of micro-magazines at a computer terminal,   10
and then sat at a video-viewer to read them.

He had just about finished one micro-magazine when his friend arrived with a charming girlfriend. Joe's friend apologized for being late and explained what had happened. Apparently he had arranged to meet the girl at six o'clock   15
(Hong Kong time) just outside the sea station not far from Los Angeles. The girl, who had traveled in a submarine only once before, had started out in plenty of time from Cairo but, unfortunately, had boarded a sub going toward Stockholm. She traveled as far as London before she realized this; the   20
submarine was very crowded and she could not see the names of the stations. By the time she got to Los Angeles, she was almost forty-five minutes late.

(After CP-25)

A. Say whether the following statements are true or false.
1. Joe expected to find his friend waiting at the space station.
2. He went to look for his friend in the space bar.
3. He went back to the space bar to read his micro-magazines.
4. Joe's friend lived near the sea station.
5. If the submarine had not been crowded, the girlfriend would have been able to see the names of the sea stations.

B. Answer the following questions.
1. Why did Joe radio his friend?
2. Why did he want energizing pills?
3. What did Joe do while waiting for his friend?
4. Why was the young lady late?
5. What time did the girl reach the right sea station?

J. Ed's interview should have begun at eleven o'clock, but the famous photographer was on the phone when Ed was shown into his office. Ed sat down in one of the armchairs near the window and waited. It sounded as if this was a long-distance call because, occasionally, the photographer 5 was shouting to make himself heard, and was becoming more and more impatient.

Ed had come to apply for a position as a photo-lab technician. He had seen the classified ad in the newspaper. At the moment, he was working as a clerk in the reference 10 section of a metropolitan library, but he did not enjoy the work at all. He liked the idea of doing work that he enjoyed. He loved to study books on photography, which was one of his hobbies. He even had his own darkroom for developing pictures. 15

While he was waiting for the photographer to finish the phone call, Ed picked up one of the colorful books that were lying on the coffee table in front of him. It was a book of adventure stories. He began to read one of them — a story about two Californian children who had been cut off by the 20 tide after spending the day on a deserted beach called Pirate's Cove. Ed had almost finished it by the time the famous photographer was ready to interview him.

(After CP-28)

A. Say whether the following statements are true or false.
1. Ed's interview began promptly at eleven.
2. The photographer had to shout while he was speaking on the phone because there was a lot of noise outside.
3. Ed liked his present job.
4. Ed knew a great deal about photography already.
5. Ed sat and listened to the photographer's conversation all the time.

B. Answer the following questions.
1. Why did Ed have to wait?
2. Why had Ed come to see the photographer?
3. How did he hear about the job in the photo lab?
4. Where was Ed working at present?
5. What was the story about that Ed was reading?

DICTATION PASSAGES

A. Of the four other people at our table, / two were men and two were women. / One of them was a doctor / traveling around the world for the last time, / before he would retire to a quiet country town. / The other man was an engineer / who had such a loud laugh / that I could hear it in my cabin, / which was next to his. / One of the women was a grandmother, / although she looked remarkably young. / She was on her way to visit her daughter / who had moved to Australia several years before. / The other woman was going to join her husband in Bangkok. / She only spoke / when she wanted to consult the doctor / about her children's ailments.

(After CP-3)

B. First of all, / I waded downstream to the place where our boat was tied up / in the shelter of some overhanging bushes. / I then rowed the boat back to the old bridge, / where the water was shallow. / We loaded it with the food, blankets / and other things that we needed. / It took about half an hour. / Dawn was just breaking / as we pulled off from the bank. / When we reached the woods three hours later, / we decided to go ashore for lunch. / I tied up the boat / while the other boys gathered wood for the fire. / Unfortunately, / although they found plenty of wood, / we could not light a fire after all. / We had forgotten to bring the matches.

(After CP-4)

C. A young woman was waiting at the bus stop / with her small suitcase beside her on the sidewalk. / She kept glancing anxiously at her watch. / Her train left at two-thirty / and it was already ten after two. / She did not want to miss her train. / So, / although taxi fare to the station / was more than she could afford, / she decided to call a taxi / from a phone at her friend's house. / She had already walked quite a way / in the direction of the friend's house / when a bus came into view. / She immediately ran back to the bus stop, / and managed to catch the bus / which, fortunately, had stopped to leave some passengers off.

(After CP-7)

D. One day when I got home, / tired after a day's shopping, / I found I had lost my purse. / I immediately retraced my steps / as far as the drugstore on Date Street, / where I had bought some cough medicine. / But there was no sign of my purse anywhere, / at least not in the streets or on the sidewalks. / Fortunately there was not much money in it, / only some small change. / But it also contained a photograph of my daughter, / taken when she was only twelve years old, / which I was very fond of / and always carried with me. / I finally went to the police station / to ask if the purse had been found. / I was happy to learn / that someone had handed it in. / The police officer had made a note of the man's name and address, / so I was able to write and thank him.

(After CP-11)

E. I went last summer / to spend my vacation on the coast. / Just before the train reached the station, / I took my suitcases down / and carried them to the end of the car. / After I had done this, / I stood by the open window, / breathing in the fresh ocean air. / Imagine my surprise / when a familiar voice greeted me. / It was my neighbor! / He was not only going to the same resort town, / but also, as I soon discovered, / had chosen the same motel to stay in. / It was an amazing coincidence.

(After CP-12)

F. In our grandfather's house / there was an attic / which was always kept locked. / One day, however, / my sister found the key in a drawer, / so we excitedly ran up the stairs / to explore the locked room. / When we managed to open the door, / we could not see anything at first. / Then I noticed a small end window / high up on a wall. / It was so covered with dust / that it did not let much light in. / I let in more light / by climbing up on a box / and cleaning the window with a rag. / But we found nothing very interesting. / Even the large box / which I was standing on / contained only business records.

(After CP-15)

G. As I was walking down the street the other day, / my curiosity was aroused by a small crowd / which had gathered near the entrance to the park. On crossing the street, / I discovered that the center of attraction / was an old man with a performing monkey. / The monkey's tricks were so spectacular / that the hat, / which the old man had placed on the sidewalk, / was soon filled with coins, / even a few dollar bills. / It seemed like an awfully easy way to make a living.

(After CP-17)

H. As soon as the ship began to turn around, / most of the passengers left the dining room / and rushed up on deck. / There they found / that a lifeboat had been lowered into the ocean. / An officer shouted an order / to the four sailors who manned the oars, / and they began to row in the direction of the man / who had been seen floating in the water. / After what seemed like ages, / they reached the man, / pulled him on board / and rowed back to the ship. / The lifeboat was raised out of the water, / and the rescued man, wrapped in a blanket, / was carried to the ship's hospital.

(After CP-19)

I. The cry seemed to come / from the trees at the far end of my yard. / I stood by the window and listened. / Again I heard the cry. / It sounded as if someone were in trouble, / so I decided to go out and have a look in the yard. / Since it was getting dark, / I armed myself with a flashlight and my son's baseball bat. / With these, I examined the far end of the yard / and the lower branches of the trees. / But there was no sign of anybody or anything. / I came to the conclusion / that one of the boys who lived in the neighborhood / was just playing a trick on me.

(After CP-21)

J. Mr. Yates was a very busy man / who expected other people to be as punctual as he was. / You can imagine how upset he was / when Mr. Becker did not show up in time / for an appointment with him / at the Becker Real Estate office.

/ Yates announced to the receptionist in Mr. Becker's office / that he would not only leave, / but that he had changed his mind / about buying a building on Sinclair Street. / Just as Mr. Yates was about to open the door, / a new employee by the name of Blake / jumped to his feet and offered to discuss the building with him. / For some reason, / Yates agreed to talk with Blake instead of Becker.

(After CP-23)

K. I will never forget the time I traveled to Mars. / I had actually intended to go to the moon / but I became confused in the launching area / because of the huge crowds of students / who were taking advantage of the summer rates. / What happened is / I was shoved into a line / which ended up in a briefing room full of Mars-bound passengers. / Strangely enough, / I sat through two hours of lectures on space travel / without realizing that I would not be going to the moon. / It wasn't until we had achieved the initial orbit around Earth / that I discovered the fact / that I was going to spend the next two years / on a voyage to and from Mars.

(After CP-24)

L. After lunch / the two boys set off toward Pirate's Cove / which was on the other side of the rocks. / It was like discovering a new world. / They explored innumerable caves, / half expecting to come across smugglers there. / They looked for fish and other strange creatures / in the small pools among the rocks. / They examined all the objects / that had been washed up by the tide. / In this way the afternoon passed quickly, / and the sun was already beginning to go down / when they reluctantly decided to head back home.

(After CP-27)